Master Public Speaking

A practical, step-by-step guide to Overcome Stage Fright, Communicate Effectively, and Persuade any Audience.

Leanne Mauro

Copyright © 2025 by Leanne Mauro - All rights reserved.

The content contained within this book may not be reproduced, duplicated or transmitted without direct written permission from the author or the publisher.

Under no circumstances will any blame or legal responsibility be held against the publisher, or author, for any damages, reparation, or monetary loss due to the information contained within this book. Either directly or indirectly. You are responsible for your own choices, actions, and results.

Legal Notice:

This book is copyright protected. This book is only for personal use. You cannot amend, distribute, sell, use, quote or paraphrase any part, or the content within this book, without the consent of the author or publisher.

Disclaimer Notice:

Please note the information contained within this document is for educational and entertainment purposes only. All effort has been executed to present accurate, up to date, and reliable, complete information. No warranties of any kind are declared or implied. Readers acknowledge that the author is not engaging in the rendering of legal, financial, medical or professional advice. The content within this book has been derived from various sources. Please consult a licensed professional before attempting any techniques outlined in this book.

By reading this document, the reader agrees that under no circumstances is the author responsible for any losses, direct or indirect, which are incurred as a result of the use of the information contained within this document, including, but not limited to, — errors, omissions, or inaccuracies.

Contents

Introduction	7
1. CONQUERING STAGE FRIGHT AND BUILDING CONFIDENCE	11
Understanding Your Fear: The Psychology Behind Stage Fright	12
Breathing and Relaxation Exercises to Calm Nerves	13
Breathing & Relaxation Exercises	14
Progressive Muscle Relaxation (PMR) Steps	18
Mindfulness Meditation	20
Visualization Techniques for Calmness, Focus, and Confident Speaking	22
Visualization Exercise: Designing Your Speaking Success	23
Reframing Negative Thoughts to Positive Outcomes	26
Cognitive Reframing Action Steps	28
Transforming Nervous Energy into Dynamic Presence	30
Power Poses, Stretching and Breathing: Transform your Nervous Energy into a Powerful Presence	31
Building a Pre-Speech Routine for Success	33
2. CRAFTING CAPTIVATING SPEECHES	35
Structuring Your Speech with the Hero's Journey	36
The Hero's Journey Roadmap	37
Applying the Structure to a Speech Theme	38
Using the Three-Act Structure for Impactful Speeches	40
Building a Solid Introduction	44
Crafting an Unforgettable Conclusion	47
Incorporating Relatable Anecdotes and Examples	51
Using Humor to Enhance Engagement	53
Crafting Memorable Messages with Emotional Resonance	55

The Role of Conflict and Resolution in Stories	56
Storytelling Checklist	57

3. DESIGNING EFFECTIVE PRESENTATION STRUCTURES — 61
- Checklist for Creating a Presentation Outline — 63
- Utilizing Templates for Consistency and Clarity — 64
- Integrating Data and Facts Seamlessly — 65
- Enhancing Engagement through Visual Storytelling — 66
- Adapting Your Structure for Different Formats — 68

4. ENGAGING AND PERSUADING YOUR AUDIENCE — 71
- Concluding with a Powerful Call to Action — 74
- Building Rapport with Diverse Audiences — 75

5. NAVIGATING QUESTIONS AND AUDIENCE INTERACTION — 78
- Techniques for Managing Unexpected Questions — 80
- Encouraging Audience Participation — 81
- Handling Difficult or Hostile Questions — 83
- Building Rapport Through Interactive Exercises — 84
- Using Feedback Loops to Enhance Engagement — 86

6. MASTERING VOCAL DYNAMICS AND BODY LANGUAGE — 90
- Exercises to Master Vocal Variety — 90
- Exercises for Improving Vocal Clarity — 92
- The Power of Pause: Using Silence Effectively — 95
- Eliminate Filler Words for Clear Impactful Speech — 96
- Body Language Essentials for Speakers — 97
- Enhancing Stage Presence Through Movement — 99
- The Role of Facial Expressions in Communication — 100

7. AUTHENTICITY AND PERSONAL BRANDING — 102
- Building a Personal Brand Through Public Speaking — 104
- Aligning Your Message with Core Values — 106
- Overcoming Imposter Syndrome with Cognitive Restructuring — 107
- Cultivating Emotional Intelligence as a Speaker — 109

8. GENDER-SPECIFIC COMMUNICATION
   STRATEGIES   111
   Empowering Female Voices: Overcoming
   Stereotypes   113
   Leveraging Male Strengths: Authenticity and
   Authority   114
   Gender-Inclusive Language: Reaching a Broader
   Audience   116
   Balancing Assertiveness and Approachability   117

9. DIGITAL VS. IN-PERSON SPEAKING TECHNIQUES   120
   Engaging Virtual Audiences: Techniques for Online
   Interaction   122
   Adapting Body Language for the Camera   124
   Bridging the Gap: Transitioning Between Digital and
   In-Person   125
   Utilizing Technology: Tools for Effective
   Presentation Delivery   127
   Managing Technical Difficulties with Poise   128

10. LEVERAGING PUBLIC SPEAKING FOR CAREER
    ADVANCEMENT   131
    Networking Through Speaking Engagements   133
    Crafting an Elevator Pitch that Stands Out   135
    Public Speaking for Professional Growth and
    Recognition   136
    Transforming Public Speaking Skills into Career
    Assets   138

11. EMBRACING CONTINUOUS IMPROVEMENT AND
    LIFELONG LEARNING   141
    Creating a Personal Development Plan for Speaking   143
    Utilizing Feedback for Continuous Improvement   145
    Staying Updated with Latest Public Speaking Trends   146
    Engaging with Public Speaking Communities for
    Growth   147
    Celebrating Milestones on Your Speaking Journey   149

    Conclusion   153
    References   157

Introduction

Picture this: a seasoned executive stands before a packed auditorium, palms sweaty, heart racing. Yet, as he begins to speak, a transformation occurs. The fear fades, replaced by confidence that captivates the audience. This isn't magic—it's the power of effective public speaking. A skill that can change careers, open doors, and inspire change.

Welcome to "Master Public Speaking: A Practical, Step-by-Step Guide to Overcome Stage Fright, Communicate Effectively, and Persuade Any Audience." My vision for this book is simple: to empower you to become a confident public speaker. You'll learn to conquer your fears and connect with any audience through practical steps and actionable strategies. Whether presenting to a boardroom or speaking at a community event, this book aims to transform your public speaking journey.

What sets this book apart is its unique features. It offers gender-specific advice, recognizing that men and women may have different approaches to public speaking. In light of the increasing importance of virtual communication, it provides insights into the differences

 between digital and in-person presentations. Additionally, real-life examples illustrate how various individuals have transformed their speaking challenges into successes. The inclusion of checklists, expert insights and practical exercises ensures that you have a comprehensive toolkit at your fingertips.

This book is for you—the adult endeavoring to elevate your public speaking skills. Whether you're a business professional, leader, entrepreneur, or coach, this guide is your roadmap to success. You'll find it invaluable for career advancement and personal growth, equipping you to lead confidently and clearly.

Why focus on public speaking? It can transform your career and boost your leadership abilities. It builds personal confidence and helps you communicate your ideas effectively and persuasively. Mastering public speaking isn't just about speaking; it's about listening, understanding your audience, and creating meaningful connections.

The structure of this book follows a logical progression. We begin by addressing stage fright and offer strategies to manage nerves and anxiety. Next, we delve into crafting your speech, exploring various storytelling techniques and methods. We then ensure clear and compelling delivery of your speech by learning vocal modulation and effective body language. Finally, we explore leveraging these skills for career advancement and personal growth.

Public speaking is a journey, not a destination. It's a skill that requires continuous improvement and practice. As you read through the chapters, remember that each step brings you closer to becoming the speaker you aspire to be. This book encourages you to embrace this journey, celebrating each milestone you achieve.

Let me conclude with a quote from the renowned public speaker and author Ralph Waldo Emerson: "All the great speakers were bad speakers at first." This quote reminds us that even the best began somewhere. With dedication and the right tools, you, too, can transform into a great speaker.

So, are you ready to take the first step on this journey? Let's begin.

Chapter 1

Conquering Stage Fright and Building Confidence

Standing at the podium, you might feel like your heart has a mind of its own, pounding loudly enough for everyone in the room to hear. We've all experienced this, it's a common feeling even among the most seasoned speakers. Consider the story of a top executive who froze during a crucial presentation, despite having years of experience. He was reminded of his first public speaking endeavor. However, this time he had learned not just how to overcome stage fright, but how to embrace it and use it to enhance his delivery.

This chapter serves as your guide to that transformation. Public speaking isn't about eliminating fear; it's about managing it and building confidence. We will explore the roots of stage fright, understand its psychological and physiological aspects, and equip you with strategies to turn anxiety into your greatest ally.

Understanding Your Fear: The Psychology Behind Stage Fright

Stage fright is a universal phenomenon, a mix of emotions that can grip anyone who steps in front of an audience. At its core, it's the fear of judgment or criticism. This anxiety often stems from a deep-seated apprehension about how others perceive us. "Will they like what I have to say?" "What if they think I'm not good enough?". Such thoughts can spiral into perfectionism, where the fear of failure looms large, making every word and gesture feel like a high-stakes gamble. There's also the fear of the unknown. Unpredictability in an audience's reaction can send shivers down your spine, especially when addressing a large crowd or those with perceived authority. This fear is not only natural but also deeply ingrained in our psyche.

Reflecting on past experiences can be revealing. Many of us carry memories of speaking engagements that didn't go to plan. Perhaps an embarrassing incident still lingers in your mind, fuelling anxiety about future performances. Whatever your triggers might be, it's crucial to identify them, not to dwell on them, but to understand and overcome them. This way, they hold less power over us.

Biologically, fear activates the fight-or-flight response, a mechanism designed to keep us safe from threats. This response can manifest as an adrenaline rush, causing symptoms like a racing heart, sweating, or shaking. Although these reactions happen to protect us, they can impede our performance when presenting to an audience. Understanding these physiological responses helps manage them, turning the adrenaline into an asset rather than a hindrance.

Knowing that stage fright affects even the most experienced speakers is comforting. Even the pros have their moments of doubt. Acclaimed author and speaker Mark Twain once admitted, "There are two types of speakers: those that are nervous and those that are liars." Knowing you're not alone can be reassuring. It's a shared human experience - one that connects us in our vulnerability and determination to communicate. Acknowledging this universality can be empowering, reminding you that stage fright is not a barrier but a bridge to more effective and engaging public speaking.

Breathing and Relaxation Exercises to Calm Nerves

The moment before you step onto stage—or even stand up from your chair in a meeting—can be fraught with tension. But here's a secret: controlled breathing is your ally. It's not just about filling your lungs with air but finding a rhythm that soothes the mind and body. This is where diaphragmatic breathing comes in. Also known as "belly breathing," this technique encourages the use of the diaphragm, the muscle located at the base of the lungs, to draw in deeper, more efficient breaths. Your belly should rise as you inhale, and as you exhale, it should fall. This practice calms your nerves and enhances oxygen flow, steadying your heartbeat and reducing anxiety. Picture a leaf gently floating down a stream—that's the serenity diaphragmatic breathing can bring.

Another excellent breathing method to consider is box breathing, a technique often used by Navy SEALs to maintain calm under pressure. Imagine drawing a square with your breath: inhale deeply for four counts, hold the breath for four counts, exhale for four counts, and pause for four counts before repeating. This structured breathing pattern creates a sense of stability and control, anchoring you in the present moment and helping to quiet the mind. It's a simple yet powerful exercise you can practice anywhere, whether in the comfort of your home or waiting to address a room full of people.

An effective exercise to further release tension is engaging in progressive muscle relaxation. Begin by tensing each muscle group in your body, one at a time, from your toes to your head, holding the tension for a few seconds before releasing. This process helps to identify and reduce physical stress, promoting a state of relaxation that can support a calm and composed demeanor. It's a way of reminding your body that it's okay to let go.

Incorporating mindfulness into your daily routine is a game-changer. Mindfulness meditation involves focusing your attention on the present moment with an attitude of openness and acceptance, acknowledging thoughts and feelings without judgment. By setting aside just a few minutes each day to sit quietly and observe your breath, you cultivate a sense of peace that can carry over into your speaking engagements. Similarly, body scan exercises can help you become more aware of physical sensations, allowing you to address and release areas of tension.

These relaxation techniques do more than calm the nerves—they sharpen focus and enhance performance. When your mind is clear, your thoughts flow more freely, and your words have a greater impact. Relaxation also improves vocal control, allowing you to project confidence and authority. As you practice these techniques, you'll find that the clarity and composure they bring extend beyond the podium, enriching every aspect of your life.

Breathing & Relaxation Exercises

Diaphragmatic Breathing

Simple steps for effective diaphragmatic breathing:

1. Find a Comfortable Position

- Sit upright in a chair or lie down, ensuring your body is supported and relaxed.

- Alternatively, take a moment before walking on stage or entering a meeting room.

2. Relax Your Body

- Place one hand on your chest and the other on your abdomen, just below your ribcage.
- Relax your shoulders and jaw.

3. Focus on Your Breathing

- Close your eyes if it helps you concentrate.
- Inhale deeply through your nose, directing your breath toward your abdomen so that your belly rises. Your chest should remain relatively still.
- Exhale slowly and completely through your mouth, gently contracting your abdominal muscles to push the air out.

4. Maintain a Regular Rhythm

- Keep the breath smooth and consistent. Avoid straining or forcing your breath.
- Gradually aim for a slower, deeper rhythm as you practice.

5. Practice Consistently

- Begin with 5 minutes a day and gradually increase the duration.

Box Breathing

Simple steps for effective box breathing:

1. Find a Comfortable Position

- Sit upright in a chair or lie down, ensuring your body is supported and relaxed.
- Rest your hands on your thighs or stomach, and allow your shoulders to relax and drop away from your ears.
- Alternatively, take a moment before walking on stage or entering a meeting room.

2. Relax and Center Yourself

- Close your eyes or soften your gaze.
- Take a few natural breaths to calm your mind and prepare for the exercise.

3. Follow the Box Breathing Pattern

Box breathing involves four equal phases. Each phase lasts for the same count (e.g., 4 seconds). Here's how to do it:

Step 1: Inhale
Breathe in deeply and slowly through your nose for a count of 4, filling your lungs fully.
Focus on expanding your abdomen and lungs.

Step 2: Hold Your Breath
Hold your breath for a count of 4, keeping your body relaxed.

Step 3: Exhale
Exhale slowly and completely through your nose for a count of 4.
Feel your lungs empty and your body relaxing.

Step 4: Hold Again
Pause and hold your breath for a count of 4 before starting the next inhale.
Stay calm and centered during this pause.

4. Repeat the Cycle

- Continue the box breathing cycle (inhale-hold-exhale-hold) for 4-6 rounds or as long as it feels comfortable.
- If 4 seconds feels too long, shorten the count to 3 or even 2 seconds, gradually increasing as you build comfort.

5. Return to Normal Breathing

- After completing your session, take a few natural breaths and notice how you feel.
- Open your eyes and return to your space. You are now ready to take on your activity with a sense of calm and focus.

Tips for Effective Practice

- Start small: Practice for 1-2 minutes per day. Gradually extend the duration as you become more comfortable.
- Stay consistent: Practice daily to experience the full benefits of box breathing.
- Adjust the count: Customize the duration of each phase to suit your lung capacity and comfort level.

Box breathing is a powerful tool you can use anytime to center yourself or manage stress.

Progressive Muscle Relaxation (PMR) Steps

Simple steps for effective progressive muscle relaxation:

1. Preparation

- Find a Quiet Space: Choose a calm, comfortable environment where you won't be disturbed.
- Get Comfortable: Sit in a chair with good back support, or lie down on a bed or mat. Alternatively, take a few moments before entering onto stage or a meeting. Rest your hands by your sides.
- Relax Your Body: Close your eyes and take a few deep breaths to settle your mind.

2. Focus on Your Breathing

- Begin by taking slow, deep breaths. Inhale deeply through your nose, hold for a moment, then exhale through your mouth.
- Imagine tension leaving your body with each exhale.

3. Start with Your Feet

- Tense: Curl your toes downward and hold the tension for about 5 seconds.
- Relax: Release the tension suddenly and focus on the sensation of relaxation for 5 seconds.
- Notice the difference between tension and relaxation.

4. Move Up Your Body

Work systematically through the following muscle groups, tensing and relaxing each one. Spend 5 seconds tensing, followed by 5 seconds relaxing:

- Calves: Point your toes downwards, tensing your calf muscles.
- Thighs: Squeeze your thighs together tightly.
- Glutes: Tighten your buttocks.
- Abdomen: Suck in your stomach, as if pulling your navel toward your spine.
- Chest: Take a deep breath and hold it, tightening your chest.
- Arms: Clench your fists and tense your forearms, then your upper arms.
- Shoulders: Shrug your shoulders up toward your ears.
- Neck: Press your head gently back into the surface or forward to stretch your neck muscles.
- Face: Scrunch your facial muscles (forehead, eyes, mouth), then relax.

5. Focus on Relaxation

- Once you've worked through all the muscle groups, spend a few moments noticing the overall sense of relaxation.
- Allow your body to remain in this relaxed state for a minute or two while breathing deeply.

Tips for Effective PMR

- Go Slow: Take your time with each muscle group to fully experience the relaxation.
- Avoid Pain: Never tense muscles to the point of pain. Aim for gentle tension.
- Practice Regularly: Practice PMR daily or whenever you feel stressed.
- Customize the Order: Modify the sequence to focus on areas where you carry the most tension.

Mindfulness Meditation

Simple steps for effective mindfulness meditation:

1. Choose a Quiet Space

- Find a calm and comfortable environment where you won't be disturbed.
- Minimize distractions by silencing your phone or other devices.

2. Get into a Comfortable Position

- Sit in a chair with your back upright and feet flat on the ground, or sit cross-legged on a cushion.
- Rest your hands on your thighs or in your lap.

3. Set an Intention

- Decide how long you'll meditate (e.g., 5, 10, or 20 minutes).
- Consider a simple intention, such as "I will focus on my breath" or "I will observe my thoughts without judgment."

4. Focus on Your Breathing

- Close your eyes or keep them softly focused on a point in front of you.
- Take a few deep breaths, inhaling through your nose and exhaling through your mouth.
- Transition to natural breathing and focus on the sensation of your breath entering and leaving your nostrils or the rise and fall of your chest or abdomen.

5. Observe the Present Moment

- Bring your attention to the here and now.
- Notice physical sensations, sounds, or the rhythm of your breath without trying to change anything.

6. Acknowledge Distracting Thoughts

- When your mind wanders (and it will), gently acknowledge the distraction without judgment.
- Use a mental cue like "thinking" or "wandering" to label the thought, then redirect your focus back to your breath or the present moment.

7. Incorporate a Focus Point (Optional)

- If helpful, use a mantra, word, or phrase (e.g., "so hum", "calm" or "I am breathing in, I am breathing out") to anchor your attention.
- Alternatively, focus on physical sensations, like the feeling of your feet on the ground or your hands resting in your lap.

8. Practice Acceptance

- Embrace whatever arises in your mind, whether it's calmness, restlessness, or emotional discomfort.
- Let go of any need to control or suppress your thoughts.

9. End with Awareness

- When your time is up, take a few deep breaths before opening your eyes.
- Reflect on how you feel and acknowledge the time you've taken for yourself.

10. Practice Regularly

- Start with short sessions (5-10 minutes) and gradually increase the duration.
- Aim to practice daily to build mindfulness as a habit.

Tips for Success

- Be Patient: It's normal for your mind to wander; what matters is bringing it back gently.
- Stay Curious: Approach each session with a beginner's mind, noticing things as if for the first time.
- Consistency Over Perfection: Even short, imperfect sessions are beneficial.

Visualization Techniques for Calmness, Focus, and Confident Speaking

Imagine standing in front of an audience, your words flowing seamlessly, and your message resonating with every listener. Your message doesn't just reach the audience; it strikes a chord, leaving an indelible mark. This isn't just a daydream—it's a potential reality you can achieve through the art of visualization. Much like elite athletes who mentally rehearse their victories before stepping onto the field, you too can employ this technique to elevate your public speaking. By harnessing the power of visualization, you create a mental rehearsal that not only diminishes anxiety but significantly enhances your confidence. This practice allows you to construct a detailed mental blueprint for success, where every aspect of your presentation, from the opening statement to the concluding applause, is meticulously crafted and envisioned in your mind's eye. Athletes have long used visualization to enhance performance, picturing themselves executing the perfect move before they even set foot on the field.

As part of your visualization practice, you can picture the venue—whether it's a grand auditorium or a small conference room—and familiarize yourself with the space. You can visualize the audience, perhaps their attentive faces, nodding in agreement as you speak. You can see yourself delivering your content smoothly, with the kind of poise and presence that captivates. You can also imagine your final moment when you finish, and the room erupts in applause, reinforcing a successful outcome.

The more you visualize your chosen images and scenarios, incorporating the feelings of a successful outcome, the more neural pathways in your brain are created and the more likely you are to have a real-life experience of a successful outcome.

To make your visualization vivid and real, engage all your senses. Smell the air in the room, perhaps tinged with the faint aroma of coffee. Hear the audience's murmur settling in their seats, the rustle of programs. Feel the warmth of the spotlight or the coolness of the microphone in your hand. The more details you can incorporate, the more your mind will accept this scenario as reality. Like a director crafting a film scene, you can set the stage for a positive speaking experience, convincing your mind that you are ready.

Visualization Exercise: Designing Your Speaking Success

Simple steps for effective visualization:

1. Create a Quiet Environment

- Find a calm, distraction-free space to focus.

- Sit or lie down in a comfortable position, close your eyes, and take a few deep breaths to relax.

2. Set a Clear Intention

- Define what you want to achieve with your speech (e.g. engage the audience, convey key messages, or inspire action).
- Imagine yourself succeeding in those goals.

3. Picture the Setting

- Visualize the venue or setting where you will speak.
- Imagine the layout, lighting, seating arrangement, and audience.
- Familiarizing yourself with the environment to mentally reduce surprises.

4. See Yourself as Confident and Prepared

- Picture yourself walking onto the stage or to the podium with confidence and poise.
- Imagine yourself standing tall, smiling, and making eye contact with the audience.
- Visualize yourself delivering your speech smoothly, articulating clearly, and connecting with the audience.

5. Imagine Audience Engagement

- Picture the audience listening attentively, nodding in agreement, smiling, or responding positively to your points.
- Visualize them clapping or expressing appreciation at the end.

6. Focus on Key Moments

- Identify critical parts of your presentation, such as the introduction, key points, or conclusion.
- Mentally rehearse delivering these moments powerfully and effectively.

7. Address Potential Challenges

- Anticipate potential challenges, such as a technical issue or a difficult question.
- Visualize yourself handling these situations calmly and effectively, maintaining composure.

8. Engage All Senses

- Imagine the sound of your voice, the feel of the microphone, the warmth of the lights, or the texture of the podium.
- Engage all your senses to make the visualization more vivid and impactful.

9. Affirm Positive Outcomes

- Repeat affirmations like, "I am well-prepared, confident, and capable," or, "My audience values my message."
- Focus on feelings of success, accomplishment and gratitude.

10. Revisit Regularly

- Practice visualization daily leading up to the event.
- The more often you mentally rehearse, the more natural and confident you'll feel during the actual presentation.

Benefits of Visualization for Public Speaking

- Builds Confidence: It prepares your mind for success and reduces performance anxiety.
- Enhances Memory: It reinforces the structure and content of your speech.
- Improves Delivery: It enhances your performance by mentally rehearsing smooth transitions and an engaging delivery.
- Promotes Resilience: By visualizing a successful navigation of challenges it helps you stay composed under pressure.

Visualization can be your mental warm-up, preparing you for any speaking challenge. As you integrate this technique, you'll find that confidence becomes a natural part of your preparation.

Reframing Negative Thoughts to Positive Outcomes

It's common to find ourselves trapped in a loop of negative thinking, especially when facing the daunting task of speaking in public. Cognitive reframing is a powerful tool that can shift your mindset from doubt to confidence. This process involves changing how you view your public speaking experiences and potential outcomes. Instead of picturing a sea of critical faces or imagining a stumble over words, cognitive reframing encourages you to replace these catastrophic thoughts with more realistic ones. Consider the difference between thinking, "I'm going to forget everything and embarrass myself," versus, "I am well-prepared, and it's okay if I pause to remember my points." By practicing this shift, you transform the narrative from impending failure to a balanced perspective, acknowledging the possibility of success and the normalcy of minor hiccups.

Recognizing when you're engaging in negative self-talk is the first step toward reframing. We often don't realize how harshly we speak to ourselves, especially in high-pressure situations. Journaling can be an effective technique to uncover these patterns. Spend a few minutes each day writing down your thoughts about public speaking. Pay attention to recurring themes or words that signal negativity. Once identified, these thoughts can be challenged and altered. Ask yourself if there's evidence to support these fears or if they stem from a place of doubt. This self-awareness is crucial for change.

To build a new, positive narrative, develop personalized affirmations. These are statements that reflect your goals and strengths as a speaker. Craft affirmations that resonate with you, such as "I communicate clearly and confidently" or "My message is valuable and well-received." Repeating these daily, especially before speaking engagements, can reinforce a positive mindset. It's not about ignoring challenges but about fostering a belief in your ability to overcome them.

Consider the story of a public speaker who once struggled with severe anxiety before every presentation. He gradually built confidence by identifying his negative thought patterns and consistently using positive affirmations. He would remind himself, "I have prepared thoroughly, and I connect well with my audience." Over time, this shift in thinking translated into more assured performances. His success wasn't immediate, but through persistent reframing, he transformed his fear into self-belief.

These stories and techniques show that cognitive reframing isn't just about thinking happy thoughts—it's about equipping yourself with a realistic, empowering outlook. It acknowledges challenges while affirming your capacity to meet them. This mindset change can be the difference between dreading the podium and embracing the opportunity to share your voice.

Cognitive Reframing Action Steps

1. Recognize Negative Self-Talk

- Pay attention to internal thoughts before and during your speech preparation.
- Identify common negative patterns, such as:
    - "I'm going to mess up."
    - "The audience won't like me."
    - "I'm not good at public speaking."

2. Challenge Negative Thoughts

- Ask yourself:
    - "Is this thought true?"
    - "What evidence supports or contradicts it?"
    - "What's the worst that could happen, and how likely is that?"

3. Replace with Constructive Thoughts

- Reframe negative thoughts into neutral or positive ones:
    - Negative: "I'll forget what I'm supposed to say."
    - Reframe: "If I lose my place, I can pause, check my notes, and continue confidently."

4. Use Positive Affirmations

- Develop affirmations that counteract your specific fears.
- Keep them short, positive, and present-tense. Examples:
    - "I am prepared and confident."
    - "I connect with my audience effortlessly."
    - "I communicate my ideas clearly and effectively."
- Repeat them daily, especially before your speech.

5. Focus on Your Purpose

- Shift your attention from yourself to the value you provide to the audience.
- Replace self-critical thoughts with audience-focused affirmations:
    - "I'm here to share something valuable."
    - "My audience is here to learn and grow with me."

6. Accept Imperfection

- Reframe perfectionism with self-compassion:
    - Negative: "I have to be flawless."
    - Reframe: "I can make mistakes and still deliver a valuable presentation."

7. Actively Seek Feedback

- Use feedback as a learning opportunity rather than a judgment.
- Replace fear of criticism with growth-focused affirmations:
    - "Each presentation makes me a better speaker."

Practical Example of Reframing and Affirmations

- Negative Thought: "What if I freeze and forget my lines?"
- Reframed Thought: "It's okay to pause. I can use my notes to refocus."
- Affirmation: "I stay calm and composed, even when unexpected challenges arise."

Transforming Nervous Energy into Dynamic Presence

Nervous energy often feels like a restless companion, eager to disrupt your composure just when you need it most. Rather than viewing it as an enemy, consider it a powerful source of vitality waiting for you to channel it. Imagine the adrenaline coursing through your veins as a tool that you can redirect from anxiety into enthusiasm. This shift in perspective can transform the way you approach public speaking. Instead of battling nerves, harness them to fuel your presence. This energy can infuse your speech with passion, turning what once felt like a hindrance into a dynamic advantage. Picture the excitement of a child before a school play—that's the kind of energy you can tap into.

Engaging in physical activity before speaking, coupled with a centered breath, can be incredibly effective in converting anxiety into focused energy. Physical exercises help to release pent-up nervousness, directing it into concentration and presence. Consider starting with a few simple stretches. These can be as straightforward as reaching for the sky or touching your toes, movements that ease muscle tension and promote relaxation. Stretching routines prepare your body and signal to your mind that it's time to focus. Another strategy is to use "power poses," as social psychologist Amy Cuddy suggests, which are stances that exude confidence and stability. Standing tall with your feet firmly planted and arms open can send powerful signals to your brain, reinforcing a sense of empowerment. This posture change can profoundly impact your mental state, preparing you to face your audience with assurance.

Dynamic body language is crucial in how you and your message are perceived. Confident body language involves more than just standing tall; it's about being open and approachable. Use gestures to emphasize key points, keeping them natural and purposeful. When your body language aligns with your words, it reinforces your message, making you more persuasive and credible. A strong posture, characterized by a straight back and level chin, conveys authority and poise. It not only influences how others see you but also affects how you feel about yourself. Engaging with your audience through eye contact and expressive gestures can create a connection that words alone cannot achieve. As you practice these techniques, you'll find that nervous energy transforms into a dynamic presence that captivates and inspires.

Consider integrating these strategies into your pre-speech routine, finding what works best for you. Perhaps a quick jog around the block or a short yoga session before your presentation can help manage adrenaline levels and focus your mind. Even simple breathing exercises can complement these physical activities, grounding you in the moment. The aim is to create a balance where your body and mind work harmoniously, allowing your nervous energy to propel you forward rather than hold you back. As you refine these practices, you'll notice a shift in how you approach public speaking, viewing it not as a daunting task but as an opportunity to shine.

Power Poses, Stretching and Breathing: Transform your Nervous Energy into a Powerful Presence

1. Neck and Shoulder Roll

- Purpose: This exercise releases tension in areas where nervous energy often accumulates.
- How to Do It:
    - Slowly roll your shoulders up, back, and down in a circular motion. Repeat 5 times.
    - Roll your neck gently from side to side or in a half-circle (avoid full circles to protect your neck).
    - Pair the movements with slow, deep breaths.
- Benefit: It relaxes your upper body, promotes better posture, and prevents stiffness during your speech.

2. Forward Fold Stretch

- Purpose: This exercise grounds your energy and relaxes your body while calming your mind.
- How to Do It:
    - Stand with your feet hip-width apart.
    - Slowly bend forward at your hips, letting your arms and head hang loosely toward the floor.
    - Slightly bend your knees if needed, and sway gently side to side.
    - Hold for 15-30 seconds, then slowly roll up, vertebrae by vertebrae, to a standing position.
- Benefit: It reduces tension, encourages blood flow, and transforms nervous energy into calm focus.

3. Power Pose

- Purpose: This exercise boosts confidence and reduces stress by opening the chest and expanding your posture.
- How to Do It:
    - Stand tall with your feet shoulder-width apart.
    - Place your hands on your hips (Wonder Woman pose) or raise them above your head in a wide "V" shape or have them down by your side palms open out.
    - Hold this pose for 2 minutes, breathing deeply.
- Benefit: It encourages a sense of authority and helps you feel grounded and in control.
- To do: Watch Amy Cuddy's TED Talk, 'Your Body Language May Shape Who You Are.' It provides a great insight into the power of power poses and 'Faking it, 'til you *become* it.'

Bonus Tip: Combine with Breathing

- Pair these stretches with deep, diaphragmatic breathing to maximize relaxation and confidence.

Building a Pre-Speech Routine for Success

Imagine stepping onto the stage with a sense of calm, every nerve under control, your mind clear and focused. Establishing a consistent pre-speech routine can make this scenario your reality. Like a ritual athletes follow before a big game, a pre-speech routine creates familiarity and ease, setting the stage for success. When you follow the same steps each time you prepare to speak, your brain begins associating these actions with a state of readiness and confidence. This routine becomes a comforting ritual that grounds you and signals to your mind that you are prepared to deliver your message. Famous speakers often use rituals. Winston Churchill, for instance, was known to rehearse his speeches in the bathtub, while Steve Jobs would practice his presentations repeatedly, often in front of a mirror, to ensure every word and gesture was perfect.

To design your routine, start with a customizable checklist. Through trial and error, over time, you will find the order that best serves you. Perhaps begin by reviewing your key points, ensuring each idea is clear and concise. This reinforces your familiarity with the material and boosts your confidence. Follow this with a vocal warm-up to prepare your voice for speaking. Simple exercises like humming or reciting tongue twisters can enhance your vocal clarity and projection. Next, practice power poses to instill a sense of authority and confidence. Consider listening to empowering music that uplifts your spirits and energizes you. Which could be a favorite song or playlist to motivate and focus your mind.

Mental preparation is equally vital. Engage in mental rehearsals where you picture yourself delivering your speech smoothly and confidently. This practice not only reinforces your memory but also builds confidence. Visualizing a successful performance can help you internalize the belief that you are capable and ready. Physical warm-ups should also not be overlooked. Simple facial muscle exercises can ensure your expressions are relaxed and responsive. Stretch your mouth, move your jaw, and practice exaggerated facial expressions to loosen up. Complement these with breathing drills to center your focus and calm your nerves. Breathing deeply and slowly can ground you, providing clarity and stability as you prepare to speak.

These small steps combine to create a powerful routine that primes you for success. Each element plays a role in building your confidence and preparing you mentally, physically, and emotionally. As you develop and refine your routine, it becomes a tailored ritual that supports your unique needs and preferences. With practice, this routine will become second nature and an integral part of your speaking preparation that you can rely on repeatedly. Embrace the process and let it guide you to the confident, composed speaker you aspire to be. With a solid routine, you'll find that stepping onto the stage feels less daunting and more like an opportunity to shine.

Chapter 2

Crafting Captivating Speeches

Imagine standing in front of a room full of people, each waiting to be inspired by your words. The lights dim, and you begin to speak. The story you tell is so engaging that the audience hangs on your every word. This is the power of compelling storytelling. It's not just about conveying information; it's about connecting with your audience emotionally. Storytelling transforms complex ideas into relatable experiences. It makes abstract concepts tangible, turning dry data into vivid narratives that resonate with the audience. Think of a story as a mnemonic device—a mental anchor that helps your audience remember your message long after your presentation is over. By engaging emotions, your stories create a bond between you and the listener, making your message not just heard but felt.

There are a few crucial elements to crafting a compelling story. Characters. Conflict. And resolution. Characters and conflict drive the narrative forward, giving your audience someone to root for and a challenge to overcome. Whether it's a tale of a young entrepreneur's struggle or a leader facing a

pivotal decision, these elements create tension and interest. The resolution provides closure, offering a satisfying conclusion that ties everything together. It's in this resolution that the moral or lesson of the story shines through, leaving a lasting impression. By weaving these components seamlessly, you create a storyline that captivates and informs, ensuring your message is impactful and memorable.

Let's look at several ways you can structure your narrative.

Structuring Your Speech with the Hero's Journey

The Hero's Journey, a concept popularized by Joseph Campbell, is more than just a framework for myths and movies—it's a powerful tool for crafting captivating speeches. This particular narrative structure resonates with audiences because it mirrors the universal challenges and triumphs we all experience. In public speaking, the Hero's Journey can transform your message into a compelling narrative, making complex ideas more relatable and memorable. The journey begins with the 'call to adventure', where you introduce your audience to the central theme or challenge. This sets the stage for engagement, inviting listeners to embark on a journey with you. Next, the 'trials and tribulations' serve as supporting arguments, illustrating struggles and obstacles that enrich the narrative. These challenges create tension and intrigue, holding the audience's attention. Finally, the 'return with the boon' concludes the journey, offering a resolution that reveals the lesson or insight gained. This conclusion leaves a lasting impression, encouraging reflection and action.

Adapting the Hero's Journey to fit different topics can enhance your speech's impact. For professional growth narratives, begin with the ambition or challenge that sparked your quest for success. Share the trials you faced—perhaps a setback in your career or a pivotal decision that tested your resolve. Conclude with the wisdom gained, inspiring your audience to pursue their own goals despite obstacles. This framework can highlight resilience and transformation, offering hope and motivation for personal challenges. Steve Jobs's 2005 Stanford commencement address is a prime example of the Hero's Journey in action. Jobs begins with his 'call to adventure', recounting his early passion for technology. He shares his trials, including being fired from Apple, which tested his resolve and ultimately led to his transformation and return. His conclusion is the boon, a lesson about following your passion and trusting that the dots will connect in the future. This structure engages and inspires your audience, leaving them with a message that resonates long after your speech ends.

The Hero's Journey Roadmap

1. Call to Adventure

The 'call to adventure' step introduces a challenge, opportunity, or moment of realization that sets the story in motion.

- **Purpose in Speech**: To draw your audience in by presenting a relatable problem or a defining moment.
- **Example**:

Speech on Overcoming Fear

"Two years ago, I stood at the edge of a diving board, heart racing. The pool beneath me was just 10 feet deep, but it felt like an ocean. Fear whispered in my ear, 'You can't do this.' Yet, a voice inside dared me to jump, not just into the water, but into a life beyond fear."

2. Trials and Tribulations

The 'trials and tribulations' step delves into the obstacles, struggles, and growth the hero faces on their journey.

- **Purpose in Speech**: To show vulnerability and demonstrate resilience, allowing the audience to connect with your experience.

- **Example**:

Speech on Starting a Business:

"The first year was brutal. I worked 12-hour days, only to face rejection after rejection. My savings dwindled, and doubt crept in. One night, staring at an empty spreadsheet, I asked myself, 'Is this worth it?' That's when I realized—the only way out was through."

3. Return with the Boon

In the 'return with the boon' step, the hero returns to share the knowledge, growth, or success they've gained with others.

- **Purpose in Speech**: To provide a resolution and inspire the audience with lessons they can apply to their own lives.
- **Example**:

Speech on Personal Growth:

"Today, I stand before you not as someone without fear, but as someone who learned to move forward despite it. That leap off the diving board taught me something priceless: courage isn't the absence of fear—it's action in the face of it. And that's a lesson we all can take with us."

Applying the Structure to a Speech Theme

Here's how you might use the full framework in a speech on Breaking Through Limitations:

1. **Call to Adventure**:
   - "A year ago, I hit a wall. My work felt stagnant, and I kept thinking, 'Is this all there is?' Then, one day, I came across a book about running a marathon. I'd never run

more than a mile in my life, but something in me said, 'Why not?' That was the moment my journey began."
2. **Trials and Tribulations**:
    - "Training was grueling. I failed to complete my first 5K, sprained my ankle, and faced mornings where staying in bed seemed easier than lacing up my shoes. But every setback taught me to dig deeper, to find a strength I didn't know I had."
3. **Return with the Boon**:
    - "Crossing the finish line wasn't the end of the journey; it was the beginning of a new perspective. I learned that limits are often self-imposed. The real challenge lies not in running the race but in believing you're capable of starting."

Why This Structure Works

- Engagement: It hooks the audience with a relatable starting point.
- Emotional Resonance: Sharing struggles builds connection and trust.
- Inspiration: Ending with lessons and triumph empowers the audience to see their own potential.

You can adapt this structure to various themes—overcoming adversity, achieving success, embracing change, or fostering leadership—while keeping the focus on connecting with and inspiring your audience.

Using the Three-Act Structure for Impactful Speeches

When creating a speech that captivates, the Three-Act Structure is a classic framework that brings clarity and impact. This structure, commonly seen in plays and films, divides the narrative into three parts:

Act 1: Setup - Introduce the central theme or problem.
Act 2: Confrontation - Explore challenges and obstacles.
Act 3: Resolution - Deliver the resolution, key takeaways, or call to action.

The Three-Act Structure is a method that not only helps you structure your thoughts but also guides your audience through a coherent and engaging journey. The setup is where you lay the groundwork. It's about establishing the context, introducing the main themes, and capturing the audience's attention. Here, you set the stage, letting your listeners in on what to expect and why it matters. As you move into the confrontation, you build tension by introducing challenges or conflicts related to your topic. This middle section is where you delve into the core of your message, offering insights and exploring complexities. By the time you reach the resolution, your audience should be ready for the solutions or conclusions you present, providing them with a satisfying closure and clear takeaways.

Crafting each part of this structure requires careful attention. In the setup, focus on creating a strong opening that makes your audience lean in. Use vivid imagery or rhetorical questions to stimulate curiosity. The confrontation should deepen their engagement. Share data, anecdotes, or testimonials illustrating the stakes and the journey. This middle section is where you maintain interest by addressing the challenges head-on. Finally, in the resolution, offer your audience clear solutions or a powerful call to action. Summarize the key points and reinforce the message, leaving them with a sense of purpose and understanding. Transitions between these acts are crucial, you can use signposts to navigate from one section to the next. Alternatively, you could use rhetorical questions to serve as a bridge, prompting the audience to reflect and anticipate what's coming next.

Three Act Structure Examples

Speech on Resilience

Theme: Overcoming challenges and building inner strength.

Act 1: Setup

- *"Two years ago, I found myself staring at a letter. It was a rejection from a job I had worked tirelessly to get. I felt defeated, wondering if all my hard work had been for nothing."*

Act 2: Confrontation

- *"The months that followed weren't easy. Each new application felt heavier than the last, and each rejection stung a little more. But during this time, I started to ask myself a different question: 'What can I control?' Slowly, I began to focus on small wins—learning a new skill, reaching out for mentorship, and reworking my approach."*

Act 3: Resolution

- *"Eventually, one of those small wins turned into a big opportunity, and I landed a role that I never imagined could be mine. What I learned is that resilience isn't about avoiding failure; it's about finding the strength to keep moving forward. And that's a lesson I carry with me every day—and one I hope you will, too."*

Speech on Innovation

Theme: Embracing creativity and thinking differently.

Act 1: Setup

- *"When I was a child, I loved to tinker with gadgets. I once took apart my dad's old radio, convinced I could make it play music louder. It didn't work—and my dad wasn't thrilled—but that curiosity stayed with me."*

Act 2: Confrontation

- *"Years later, as an engineer, I faced a challenge at work that seemed impossible. Our team had to redesign a product on a tight deadline with limited resources. We tried every conventional solution, but nothing worked. Frustration was high, and doubt crept in."*

Act 3: Resolution

- *"In a moment of clarity, I remembered my childhood tinkering. I realized innovation often comes from stepping outside the box. We approached the problem with fresh eyes and tested an unconventional idea—and it worked. That experience taught me that creativity isn't about being perfect; it's about being willing to try."*

Speech on Leadership

Theme: Leading with empathy and vision.

Act 1: Setup

- *"When I was promoted to manager for the first time, I thought I had to have all the answers. I felt the weight of responsibility and wanted to prove myself to the team."*

Act 2: Confrontation

- *"But things didn't go as planned. My team struggled with a big project, and I felt the pressure mounting. Instead of collaborating, I tried to micromanage, thinking it was the only way to ensure success. This approach backfired—morale dropped, and I realized something had to change."*

Act 3: Resolution

- *"I began to listen more, asking my team for their input and ideas. I learned that leadership isn't about control; it's about empowering others. That shift not only saved our project but also created a stronger, more united team. Leadership, I've learned, is a journey of growth and connection."*

Why the Three-Act Structure Works for Speeches

- Clarity: It provides a clear flow, making your speech easy to follow.
- Engagement: It mirrors the natural rhythm of storytelling, holding the audience's attention.
- Emotional Impact: The journey from problem to solution creates resonance and inspiration.

Consider a TED Talk that masterfully employs this structure. The speaker begins with a personal anecdote that sets the context, drawing listeners into the narrative. As the talk progresses, the speaker confronts the issue by weaving in statistics and real-world examples, heightening the tension. In the final act, the speaker presents a compelling resolution, offering actionable insights and a memorable closing statement. This method keeps the audience engaged, making the speech impactful and unforgettable.

Building a Solid Introduction

The introduction of a speech is crucial—it sets the tone, captures the audience's attention, and establishes a connection with them. First impressions can determine whether listeners tune in or check out. Engaging your audience from the start ensures they're invested in your message, laying the groundwork for a successful presentation.

Here are the key points to consider when crafting a strong introduction:

1. Grab Attention Immediately

- Purpose: To hook the audience from the first moment.
- Techniques:
    - Use a powerful quote or statistic.
    - Start with a surprising fact or story.
    - Ask a thought-provoking question.
    - Begin with humor, if appropriate.
- Example:
    - Consider this: 'while the average individual dedicates 25 years to sleep, how much of our waking life is spent in pursuit of our dreams?'

2. Establish Relevance

- Purpose: To show the audience why your topic matters to them.
- How:
    - Connect your topic to their interests, challenges, or goals.
    - Use phrases like, "You might be wondering how this affects you…" or "This is relevant because…"
- Example:
    - "Whether you're a student, a professional, or an entrepreneur, we've all faced moments where fear held us back. Today, I'll show you how to overcome that fear."

3. Introduce Yourself (Briefly)

- Purpose: To establish credibility and build trust.
- How:
    - Mention your relevant expertise, experience, or connection to the topic.
    - Keep it concise; focus on the audience, not yourself.
- Example:
    - "As someone who spent five years studying resilience in the workplace, I've seen firsthand how small changes can lead to remarkable results."

4. State Your Purpose Clearly

- Purpose: To let the audience know what to expect.
- How:
    - Outline the main topic or goal of your speech.
    - Use phrases like, "Today, we'll explore…" or "By the end of this talk, you'll learn…"

- Example:
    - "Today, we'll uncover three strategies to communicate with confidence, no matter the audience."

5. Create a Roadmap

- Purpose: To provide a preview of what you'll cover.
- How:
    - Briefly mention the main points or sections.
    - Keep it engaging and concise.
- Example:
    - "We'll begin by understanding the roots of fear, move on to practical techniques for managing it, and finish with actionable steps to build lasting confidence."

6. Set the Tone

- Purpose: To align the mood of your speech with your topic.
- How:
    - Match your energy and delivery to the subject (e.g., passionate for motivational topics, calm for serious subjects).
    - Use language that reflects the desired tone.
- Example:
    - For an inspiring speech: "What if I told you that the key to unlocking your potential is already within you?"
    - For a serious speech: "Every day, millions of people face the consequences of homelessness. Today, we'll discuss what we can do to make a difference."

7. Build Curiosity or Intrigue

- Purpose: To make the audience eager to hear more.
- Techniques:
    - Use a teaser or leave an open-ended statement.
    - Pose a question that will be answered later in the speech.
- Example:
    - "What's the one habit that all successful leaders share? By the end of this talk, you'll know—and be ready to apply it."

8. Keep It Brief

- Purpose: To start strong and transition smoothly into the main content.
- How:
    - Limit your introduction to 10–15% of the total speech time.
    - Avoid overloading it with details or tangents.

By focusing on these points, you'll create an introduction that captivates your audience, establishes credibility, and sets the stage for a compelling and impactful speech.

Barack Obama's "Yes We Can" speech is an excellent example of a strong opening. It began with a powerful narrative that inspired hope and unity.

Crafting an Unforgettable Conclusion

A speech's conclusion is akin to the final note of a symphony. It's your final opportunity to leave a lasting impression on your audience. A memorable ending ties everything together, reinforces your key message, and inspires action or thought.

To create your unique conclusion, consider what you want your audience to feel, think, or do after you finish speaking. Are you aiming to inspire change, provoke thought, or simply leave your audience with a smile? Craft your conclusion to meet your audience's specific needs and interests, ensuring it resonates personally and professionally. This personal connection can transform your closing remarks into a catalyst for change, offering your listeners a clear path forward.

Here are the key points to consider when crafting an unforgettable conclusion:

1. Signal the Conclusion Clearly

- Purpose: To let the audience know you're wrapping up to focus their attention.
- How:
    - Use transition phrases like, "In conclusion," "Let me leave you with this," or "As we come to the end…"
- Example:
    - "Before I leave you today, I want to share one final thought."

2. Reinforce Your Key Message

- Purpose: To ensure your central idea is remembered.
- How:
    - Summarize your speech in one or two concise sentences.
    - Highlight the main takeaway or the "big idea."
- Example:
    - "Remember, resilience isn't about avoiding failure—it's about learning to rise stronger every time."

3. End with a Call to Action

- Purpose: To motivate your audience to take specific action or adopt a new perspective.
- How:
    - Clearly state what you want your audience to do next.
    - Tailor the call to action to your topic and audience.
- Example:
    - "Today, I challenge you to take just one small step toward the goal you've been putting off. Start now—because your future self is waiting."

4. Use a Memorable Closing Technique

- Purpose: To leave the audience with something impactful and thought-provoking.
- Techniques:
    - **Call Back to Your Opening**: Refer to a story, statistic, or question you used at the start of your speech.
        - *Example*: "Just like the diving board I mentioned earlier, every leap you take today will lead you closer to your potential."
    - **Powerful Quote**: Choose one that resonates with your message.
        - *Example*: "'The journey of a thousand miles begins with a single step.' So, take that first step today."
    - **Story or Anecdote**: Share a short, emotional story that reinforces your theme.
        - *Example*: "I'll never forget the smile on my son's face when I told him I finally finished that marathon—it reminded me that our actions inspire others more than we realize."
    - **Rhetorical Question**: Leave the audience pondering.

- *Example*: "If not now, when? And if not you, who?"

5. Appeal to Emotion

- Purpose: To create a lasting emotional connection.
- How:
    - Use vivid language, imagery, or an inspiring vision of the future.
- Example:
    - "Imagine a world where each of us steps into our full potential. It starts with a single decision—and that decision is yours to make."

6. End with Confidence

- Purpose: To leave no doubt that your speech is complete and impactful.
- How:
    - Pause briefly after delivering your final words.
    - Avoid filler phrases like "That's all I have" or "Thank you for listening."
- Example:
    - *Final words*: "The power to change is in your hands. Use it wisely."

7. Practice Brevity

- Purpose: To avoid dragging out the ending.
- How:
    - Keep your conclusion concise—no more than 10% of your total speech.

Putting It All Together: Example Conclusion

- Signal: "As I wrap up, let me leave you with this thought."
- Reinforce Key Message: "Every great achievement begins with a small, courageous step."
- Call to Action: "So, be courageous and take that step today. Write down one goal, and commit to making it happen."
- Memorable Close: "Because, as the saying goes, 'What lies behind us and what lies before us are tiny matters compared to what lies within us.' Thank you."

By focusing on these key points, you can craft a conclusion that ensures your speech resonates with your audience long after it ends.

Reflect on John F. Kennedy's iconic conclusion, "Ask not what your country can do for you—ask what you can do for your country." This closing line exemplifies the power of a well-crafted ending, compelling action, and inspiring a sense of shared responsibility.

Incorporating Relatable Anecdotes and Examples

Imagine you're standing before a room filled with attentive listeners. You start with a story, a snippet of your own experience, and suddenly, you see nods of recognition. This is the magic of anecdotes in public speaking. They transform abstract concepts into tangible, relatable moments. Anecdotes can serve as compelling evidence, illustrating your points with vivid clarity. They have the power to connect your audience emotionally, making your message resonate on a personal level. Sharing a short, personal story creates a bridge between your ideas and your listener's experiences, fostering a sense of understanding and relatability that dry facts alone can't achieve.

Finding the right stories can be daunting, but it doesn't have to be. Start by mining your personal experiences. Reflect on moments in your life that taught you important lessons or shifted your perspective. These real-life anecdotes add authenticity and make your message more relatable. Additionally, consider adapting historical or cultural tales that align with your message. These stories, rich in context and meaning, can bridge the gap between speaker and audience, offering familiar themes that resonate universally. The key is ensuring these narratives align with your core message, enhancing your point rather than distracting from your point.

Selecting the right anecdotes is crucial for their effectiveness. First, consider your core message. Your story should align seamlessly with the main point, reinforcing rather than distracting from your message. Think about your audience, too. What stories will resonate with their backgrounds, interests, and experiences? An anecdote that speaks to a universal truth or shared experience can be particularly impactful. It's about striking a balance between personal relevance and broader appeal. A well-chosen story can illuminate your message, making it clearer and more memorable.

Integrating anecdotes into your speech requires finesse. Begin with one to grab attention, setting the stage for your main message. Alternatively, use them to bridge between points, providing a narrative thread that guides your listeners through your ideas. The key is to weave them in naturally, ensuring they complement, rather than interrupt, the flow of your speech.

Top 3 Tips for Incorporating Anecdotes into your Speech

1. **Make the Anecdote Relevant to Your Message.**
   Example: If your speech is about perseverance, share a story of a time you faced and overcame a significant challenge, then tie it back to the broader theme.

2. **Use Vivid Details and Emotions.** Example: Instead of saying, "I was nervous before my big presentation," say, "My palms were sweaty, my heart was pounding, and I could feel every eye in the room watching as I stepped onto the stage."
3. **Tailor the Anecdote to Your Audience.** Example: For a corporate audience, share a workplace-related story. For students, choose a school or personal growth anecdote.

Look to political campaign speeches for inspiration. Politicians often use personal stories to humanize complex policies, making them accessible and relatable to the public. These anecdotes become potent tools, transforming abstract ideas into concrete, relatable examples that stick with the audience long after the speech ends.

Using Humor to Enhance Engagement

Imagine a room full of people, the atmosphere charged with anticipation, and suddenly, a wave of laughter ripples through the crowd. That's the magic of humor in storytelling. It lightens the mood, makes your narrative more engaging, and creates a relatable bridge between you and your audience. When used effectively, humor can transform a mundane speech into a memorable experience. It breaks down barriers, making complex topics more digestible and enjoyable. Adding humor to your speech can also make your message more memorable, as people tend to remember moments that make them laugh. This doesn't mean every speech needs to be a comedy routine, but a well-placed joke or witty observation can make a big difference.

Finding humor that aligns with your personal style and audience is crucial. Observational humor draws from everyday situations and can be a great starting point. Think about those little moments in life that everyone can relate to, like the chaos of a morning commute or the quirks of office life. These relatable scenarios can elicit genuine laughter. Self-deprecating anecdotes can also be effective, as they

show humility and make you more approachable. Sharing a light-hearted story about a personal mishap can humanize you and put your audience at ease. The key is to ensure that your humor resonates with your audience's experiences and expectations.

Integrating humor seamlessly into your narrative requires a delicate balance. Timing and pacing are essential. A joke delivered too early can fall flat, while one told too late might feel out of place.

Top 3 Tips for Incorporating Humor into your Speech

1. **Keep It Relevant to Your Message.** Example: In a speech about teamwork: *"They say teamwork makes the dream work. But I've also learned that too many cooks in the kitchen just means you're ordering takeout."*
2. **Know Your Audience.** Example: For a professional audience, a witty observation about workplace dynamics might work better than a slapstick story.
3. **Use Humor Sparingly and Naturally.** Example: *"Before I started public speaking, I thought my greatest fear was heights. Turns out, it's heights... while holding a microphone!"*

Look to successful humorists like Ellen DeGeneres or Jimmy Kimmel, who masterfully weave humor into their speeches and monologues. Their ability to engage through humor without detracting from their message makes them stand out.

Crafting Memorable Messages with Emotional Resonance

Imagine the power of emotion in a speech—how the right words, delivered with sincerity, can linger in the hearts of your audience long after you've stepped away from the podium. Emotion acts as a powerful catalyst in making messages stick. When a speech stirs feelings, it taps into the brain's memory center, creating a lasting imprint. Emotional triggers activate this process, connecting your audience to the content on a deeper level, ensuring they remember your message in their minds and hearts. This emotional connection is key to making your message resonate and be impactful.

To evoke such emotions, start by weaving vivid imagery into your narrative. Paint a picture with your words that allows the audience to see, hear, and feel what you're describing. This technique immerses them in your world, making your message more relatable and engaging. Use emotional language to convey passion and conviction. Words that evoke empathy, joy, or even sorrow can touch your audience profoundly, drawing them into your message. It's about creating an emotional journey that aligns with your speech's purpose, making your audience feel like they're part of your story.

Balancing emotion with logic is crucial to maintaining credibility. While emotion engages the heart, logic appeals to the mind, providing a foundation of rationality. Integrate statistics and factual data alongside your emotional appeals to fortify your argument and demonstrate your expertise. This combination of emotion and logic is a form of ethical persuasion, as it respects the audience's intelligence while appealing to their feelings. Martin Luther King Jr.'s "I Have a Dream" speech exemplifies this balance. His use of powerful imagery and emotional language, combined with logical appeals for justice and equality, created a message that inspired change and remains timeless.

The Role of Conflict and Resolution in Stories

Conflict is the heartbeat of storytelling. Without it, narratives often fall flat, lacking the tension that keeps audiences engaged. In every compelling story, conflict introduces challenges that captivate listeners, pulling them into the drama of the narrative. This friction sparks interest, transforming a simple tale into a gripping saga. For your speeches, conflict can be as straightforward as a problem your audience faces or as intricate as a moral dilemma. When crafted well, these conflicts resonate because they reflect relatable and universal struggles. Everyone has faced personal or professional challenges, and these shared experiences can create a powerful connection with your audience.

To develop conflicts that genuinely resonate, draw from challenges that your audience might face. Think about common obstacles in your field or broader societal issues. Universal themes of struggle, such as overcoming adversity or seeking justice, can strike a chord with diverse audiences. The key is to ensure the conflict is both relevant and relatable, allowing your listeners to see themselves within the narrative. As you construct these conflicts, keep your audience in mind, crafting scenarios that are both engaging and meaningful to them.

Resolution is where the magic happens. It's the moment when tension releases, and the narrative finds its balance. It is crucial to provide a clear path from conflict to solution, as it offers your audience closure and satisfaction. Highlight the lessons learned through the resolution, reinforcing the core message of your speech. In her widely viewed TED Talk, Brené Brown doesn't just present research — she tells the story of her own emotional resistance to vulnerability. The internal conflict she experiences leads to a powerful realization that reshapes her understanding of courage and connection. Her conclusion doesn't simply summarize her message — it resolves the emotional tension of her story, leaving the audience with a clear and deeply human insight. Without conflict, her story might have lacked impact, but with it, she created a memorable and inspiring conclusion.

Storytelling Checklist

Top 5 points to ensure your speech is compelling, structured, and **impactful:**

1. Define Your Core Message

- Why it's important: Every great speech has a single, clear takeaway that resonates with the audience.
- Ask yourself:
    - What's the main idea or theme of my speech?
    - Can I summarize my speech in one sentence?
- Example: "The key to success is not talent, but resilience."

2. Understand Your Audience

- Why it's important: Tailoring your speech to the audience ensures relevance and connection.
- Ask yourself:
    - Who is my audience, and what are their interests, challenges, or needs?
    - What tone and style will resonate best with them?
- Example: For a corporate audience, focus on actionable strategies; for students, share relatable stories and encouragement.

3. Craft a Compelling Structure

- Why it's important: A clear structure helps your audience follow and remember your message.
- Structure checklist:
  - Introduction: Does it grab attention and establish relevance?
  - Body: Are the main points logically organized and supported with stories or evidence?
  - Conclusion: Does it reinforce my message and leave a lasting impression?

4. Use Storytelling Effectively

- Why it's important: Stories engage emotions, make concepts relatable, and enhance retention.
- Ask yourself:
  - Are my stories authentic and relevant to my message?
  - Do they follow a narrative arc (beginning, middle, end)?
  - Do they include vivid details and emotional resonance?
- Example: Share a personal failure and how you overcame it to illustrate resilience.

5. End with Impact

- Why it's important: The conclusion is what the audience will remember most.
- Conclusion checklist:
  - Does it reinforce my core message?
  - Is there a clear call to action or thought-provoking takeaway?
  - Does it include a memorable closing line, story, or quote?

- Example: "Remember, the only thing standing between you and your dreams is the courage to take the first step. So, take it."

BONUS TIP

Write for the Ear, Not the Eye

- Why it's important: Speeches are meant to be heard, not read, so the language should be conversational and engaging.
- Language checklist :
    - Are my sentences short and simple?
    - Have I included rhetorical devices (e.g., repetition, metaphors, questions)?
    - Does the language feel natural when spoken aloud?
- Tip: Read your speech out loud to check flow and tone.

Practice, Practice, Practice!

Mastering storytelling is not an overnight task. It's like learning a musical instrument—the more you practice, the better you become. You will find your voice and rhythm by honing this skill through repeated practice. Selecting impactful real-life stories is the first step. Choose tales that resonate with your audience—stories that align with your message and carry a clear moral or takeaway. Consider your audience's interests and what they care about. A story about overcoming adversity can be powerful if it strikes a chord with one's experiences. Clarity and relevance are your guiding principles.

To refine your storytelling abilities -

- Immerse yourself in exercises to enhance your narrative skills, such as the 'show, don't tell' drill, where you write an emotion (e.g., anger, joy, fear) without naming it. Instead you describe how it looks, feels, or sounds through action and imagery. Or try the '2-minute life story' exercise where you practice telling your own story in 2 minutes. Then try for 1 minute. Then 30 seconds. You'll learn what to keep and what to trim.
- Engage in story circles or workshops where you can share your stories and receive feedback. These environments foster creativity and offer fresh perspectives.
- Record your narratives and self assess. Listen and critique your own work, noting areas for improvement. This practice helps you identify nuances in your delivery and refine your storytelling technique.
- Gather constructive criticism from your peers. Feedback is invaluable in this process, it can illuminate blind spots and highlight strengths you might overlook.
- Consider enlisting the help of a professional storytelling coach for tailored guidance. They can offer expert advice on polishing your narratives and enhancing your delivery. This feedback loop is not just about identifying weaknesses—it's about continuous growth and development.

In storytelling, the journey of practice is where growth happens. As you develop your skills, your stories will become more vivid, engaging and powerful with each telling.

Chapter 3

Designing Effective Presentation Structures

Imagine standing before a room filled with anticipative faces, each pair of eyes locked onto you, waiting to be engaged. Every successful presentation, whether a pitch to potential investors or a motivational speech at a conference, begins with a solid foundation—a clear and logical outline. Without it, your message can become a tangled web of ideas, diminishing your impact. A well-structured outline is like a roadmap, guiding you and your audience through the intricate landscape of your presentation. It ensures that each point flows seamlessly into the next, creating a cohesive narrative that captivates and informs. Think of it as the backbone of your talk, providing the support needed to elevate your message from good to unforgettable.

A presentation outline serves as a blueprint for success. It organizes your thoughts, allowing you to highlight key points and weave them into a compelling story. By defining your objectives early on, you can focus your content and avoid the pitfalls of tangential information. This clarity not only benefits you as a speaker but also enhances the experience for your audience, who can follow your narrative with ease. A structured approach eliminates confusion, providing a clear path from introduction to conclusion. This methodology is not just about listing points; it's about creating a logical progression that builds momentum and reinforces your message.

Creating an effective outline involves a few key steps. Start by identifying your main objectives—the core message you want your audience to take away. These objectives will guide the structure of your presentation, ensuring every element serves a purpose. Next, organize your main points and sub-points, grouping related ideas under common themes. Consider using bullet points or numbering to delineate sections. Once you have these points laid out you can think about how they connect and what you can say to transition between sections of your presentation.

Transitions act as bridges between ideas and are crucial for maintaining flow. Use a transition technique such as 'signposting' to guide your audience with verbal cues such as "now that we've explored..." or "let's move on to...". This can help listeners follow along and anticipate what's coming next.

A successful outline is more than just a list—it's a dynamic tool that adapts to the needs of your presentation. For instance, an academic lecture might follow a chronological outline, guiding students through a timeline of events. This method helps in presenting complex information in a digestible format. Conversely, a business proposal might use a problem-solution structure, starting with a challenge and leading the audience to a proposed solution. This approach highlights the benefits of your proposal, making it persuasive and compelling. Each type of presentation benefits from a different method or approach, but the underlying principle remains the same: organization leads to clarity in writing and success in public speaking.

To illustrate this, let's consider a pitch deck outline of a startup. Begin with a compelling problem statement that grabs attention. Follow

with a value proposition, highlighting how your product or service addresses the problem. Detail your product's features and benefits, then discuss your business model and competitive landscape. Finally, conclude with your fundraising goals, clearly stating what you need and how it will propel your startup forward. This structured approach makes your pitch clear and engaging and positions you as a credible, confident speaker.

Checklist for Creating a Presentation Outline

- **Define Your Objectives**: Clearly state what you want your audience to learn or do.
- **Organize Main Points**: Group related ideas and ensure each point supports your core message.
- **Develop Sub-points**: Expand on main points with detailed information or examples.
- **Craft Transitions**: Create smooth connectors between sections to maintain flow.
- **Review and Revise**: Revisit your outline to ensure clarity and coherence.

Creating a strong outline is an investment in your presentation's success. It sets the stage for a narrative that informs and inspires. As you refine your outlining skills, your presentations will become more impactful, leaving a lasting impression on your audience.

Utilizing Templates for Consistency and Clarity

Imagine preparing for a presentation without the stress of starting from scratch every time. Templates are your secret weapon, offering a consistent structure streamlining the preparation process. They act like a trusty framework, ready to hold the unique content you bring. Using templates saves valuable time, allowing you to focus on refining your message rather than wrestling with formatting. This consistency enhances clarity, ensuring your audience can easily follow your narrative. Templates provide a visual standard that's easy on the eyes, making your presentation feel professional and polished. They're not just about aesthetics but about delivering your message with impact and ease.

Choosing the right template is crucial, as it must align with your content and your brand's identity. Start by considering the overall tone of your presentation. Are you aiming for a formal or casual feel? Your choice of template should reflect this. Look for designs that complement your brand colors and style. A financial report might benefit from a clean, minimalist template, while a product launch could use something more vibrant and dynamic. Customizing the layout to fit specific content is also key. You might need more space for visuals in one section and more text in another. Adjusting font sizes, colors, and slide order can make a template feel uniquely yours while maintaining its professional edge.

When it comes to tools for creating templates, you've got options. PowerPoint and Keynote are popular choices, offering flexibility and a wide range of designs to get you started. Both allow easy customization, so you can tweak templates to fit your needs perfectly. For those looking for something ready-made, online resources provide a treasure trove of templates tailored to various fields. Websites like SlideModel.com offer templates for everything from company profiles to business case studies. These resources save time and offer inspiration, ensuring your presentation stands out.

Let's look at examples of how templates transform presentations. Consider a financial report presentation: using a consistent template helps ensure that complex data is presented clearly. Each slide follows a uniform structure, making it easier for your audience to digest information. Similarly, a product launch presentation can benefit from a dynamic template that highlights key features and benefits with engaging visuals. By maintaining consistency, you reinforce your message and keep your audience engaged. Templates are more than just a tool—they're a strategic ally in your presentation arsenal. They simplify preparation, enhance clarity, and ensure your message is delivered with professionalism and impact.

Integrating Data and Facts Seamlessly

Imagine you're sitting in a meeting, and the speaker shares an impressive fact that immediately shifts your perspective. This is the power of data in presentations. It's not just about throwing numbers at your audience; it's about using these numbers to support your message and enhance your credibility. Data acts as solid evidence, backing up your claims and providing a stronger foundation for your arguments. In a world where decisions are increasingly data-driven, incorporating factual information can set you apart and lend authority to your voice. Your audience is more likely to trust what you say when they know it's grounded in reliable data.

Presenting data clearly is an art. It's about transforming complex information into something understandable and engaging, ensuring your audience doesn't get lost in the numbers. Start by simplifying your data visualizations. Avoid overwhelming your audience with too much information at once. Focus on highlighting key figures that underscore your message. A clean, uncluttered chart is more impactful than a dense spreadsheet. Use colors to differentiate data sections, highlighting the most crucial parts. Consider telling a story with your data, guiding your audience through the numbers with a narrative that links back to your main points. This approach not only clarifies your data but also keeps your audience engaged.

You'll need the right tools and techniques to create effective data presentations. Infographics are popular, offering a visually appealing way to present data. They combine images, charts, and minimal text to convey complex information. Charts and graphs are also essential in your toolkit. They provide a straightforward way to display trends, comparisons, and relationships between data points. Tools like Tableau and Google Charts are excellent for crafting these visuals, offering user-friendly interfaces and a range of customization options. Whether you're presenting sales figures or research data, these tools can help you create informative and engaging visuals.

Let's look at how data integration can transform a presentation. In scientific research presentations, data is the backbone of the argument. Researchers use data to validate their findings, often employing a mix of charts and graphs to illustrate results. This method supports their conclusions and allows the audience to visualize the impact of the research. Similarly, in business performance reports, data is crucial to demonstrating company growth or identifying areas for improvement. You can make your case more persuasive by presenting sales trends or customer demographics through clear visuals. The goal is to ensure that your audience understands the data and sees its relevance to your message.

Enhancing Engagement through Visual Storytelling

Picture yourself as an audience member in a presentation. You're listening, but your mind starts to wander. Then, a striking image appears on the screen, instantly pulling you back into the moment. This is the power of visual storytelling. Visuals do more than decorate a slide; they enhance your narrative, making complex ideas digestible and engaging. Visual storytelling is about using images, graphs, and videos to complement your spoken words, creating an immersive experience for your audience. It's the difference between telling someone about a concept and letting them see it for themselves. Visual aids are crucial because they convey information quickly and effectively, bridging the gap between the speaker and the audience.

Crafting compelling visual narratives requires a thoughtful approach. It's not just about finding pretty pictures; it's about choosing visuals that align with and amplify your message. Start by designing impactful slides that are clean and focused. Avoid clutter and unnecessary text, allowing the visuals to speak for themselves. Use metaphorical imagery to evoke emotions or clarify abstract ideas. For instance, if discussing growth, a budding plant can symbolize progress and potential. This kind of imagery can make your message more relatable and memorable. Remember, your visuals should serve the story, not distract from it. Each image or graphic should have a purpose, guiding your audience through the presentation with clarity and intent.

Integrating visuals seamlessly into your speech is an art. Timing is everything. Sync your visuals with your speech content to reinforce your points effectively. Practice your timing to ensure that each slide complements what you are saying at that moment, creating a cohesive flow. Avoid overloading your slides with too much information, as this can overwhelm your audience and detract from your message. Instead, focus on key visuals that highlight your main points. Keep transitions between slides smooth, using them to guide your audience naturally through your presentation.

Consider the impact of visual storytelling in various settings. In business pitch decks, visuals play a critical role. They illustrate the potential of a product or service and engage investors on a deeper level. A well-crafted pitch deck uses visuals to convey complex data and projections succinctly, making the case for investment compelling and clear. In scientific conference presentations, visuals help break down complex theories and results into understandable segments. Graphs, charts, and images bring the data to life, allowing the audience to grasp the significance of the research without getting bogged down in technical jargon.

Visual storytelling is a potent tool in your presentation arsenal. It enhances engagement, clarifies your message, and leaves a lasting impression. By carefully selecting and integrating visuals, you can transform your presentations into memorable experiences that resonate with your audience long after you've finished speaking.

Adapting Your Structure for Different Formats

In today's dynamic world, presentations aren't bound by a single format. The shift from traditional in-person workshops to online webinars illustrates the need for flexibility. Each setting demands its own approach. In an online webinar, you might face the challenge of engaging an audience that could be multitasking or dealing with distractions. Here, your structure might lean on engaging visuals and concise points, ensuring you maintain attention despite the digital divide. In contrast, an in-person workshop offers the luxury of physical presence, allowing for more interactive elements like group activities or live demonstrations. Your structure can be more fluid, adapting on the fly to audience reactions.

Similarly, the setting of your presentation, whether a formal conference or a casual team meeting, influences its structure. At a formal conference, your presentation needs to be polished and professional, often requiring a linear and evidence-backed approach. Here, every word matters as you're speaking to peers or industry leaders who expect depth and insight. In a casual team meeting, however, you can be more relaxed and conversational, allowing for open dialogue and spontaneous interaction. The structure might include more Q&A or brainstorming sessions to encourage participation and feedback. This adaptability is crucial in ensuring your message is effectively received, regardless of the environment.

Tailoring your content to suit diverse audience types is another aspect of this flexibility. A general audience might require you to simplify complex concepts, focusing on clarity and relatability. You might use analogies or relatable examples to bridge gaps in understanding. On the other hand, addressing an audience of experts demands depth and specificity. Here, your structure should support detailed analysis, diving into technical data or advanced theories. Understanding your audience's background and expectations helps craft a presentation that resonates, ensuring you neither overwhelm nor underwhelm.

The dynamics of interactive versus non-interactive formats also play a significant role in shaping your presentation structure. Interactive formats invite audience participation, requiring you to incorporate elements like Q&A sessions or live polls. These interactions break up the monotony and make the experience engaging and memorable. You might structure your presentation around key discussion points, allowing for back-and-forth dialogue. In non-interactive settings, where interaction is limited, your structure should focus on delivering a concise and compelling message, using rhetorical questions or storytelling to maintain interest. The choice between these formats often depends on the goals of your presentation and the needs of your audience.

Being prepared for unexpected changes in format is also essential. Technology failures, for instance, can disrupt even the most well-prepared presentations. Have a backup plan, such as printed handouts or a second device, to ensure you're not caught off guard. Adjusting your timing is another aspect of adaptability. If you're running over time, knowing which points to condense or skip can help you stay on track without losing your audience's interest. Flexibility is about pivoting smoothly, ensuring external factors don't derail your primary objectives.

In wrapping up this chapter, consider how these concepts and strategies enhance your presentations and connect you more deeply with your audience. As we move forward, think about how you can leverage these skills to boost your professional and personal growth. In the next chapter, we'll explore how public speaking can be a powerful tool to persuade and engage any audience.

Chapter 4

Engaging and Persuading Your Audience

Imagine being at a conference where the speaker steps up, begins their presentation, and, within minutes, has you hooked. Not just listening but truly engaged, nodding along. That's the power of a persuasive argument. It's not just about presenting facts; it's about weaving them into a narrative that captivates and convinces. Think about moments when you've been swayed by someone's words. It could be a pitch that convinced you to invest or a speech that inspired you to take action. These experiences highlight the effectiveness of a well-crafted persuasive argument. They're powerful because they're built on clear claims, logical reasoning, and compelling evidence—components we will explore and refine in this chapter.

Crafting persuasive arguments involves a blend of art and science. At its core, persuasion starts with a clear claim. This is your thesis, the central idea you need your audience to accept. It should be specific, assertive, and leave no room for ambiguity. Think of it as the backbone of your argument, providing structure and direction. Once you have your claim, logical reasoning comes into play. This is where you connect the dots for your audience, leading them from your claim to the conclusion you want them to reach. Use logical progression to build your case, ensuring each point flows naturally into the next. Finally, supporting evidence is your secret weapon. This could be in the form of statistics, expert testimonials, or real-world examples. It's the proof that backs up your claims, adding weight to your argument and making it more convincing. When combined, these elements create a persuasive argument that not only informs but also influences.

Organizing your argument for maximum effect requires strategy. One effective method is the problem-solution approach. Start by identifying your audience's problem, explaining its impact, and then present your solution as the ideal answer. This technique works because it taps into your audience's desire for resolution, providing a clear path from challenge to solution. Another robust framework is Monroe's Motivated Sequence, a five-step process that guides the audience from attention to action. Begin by capturing their attention with an engaging opening, then identify the problem, introduce your solution, help the audience visualize the benefits, and finally, prompt them to take action. This method is particularly effective in persuasive speeches because it taps into both logical and emotional appeals, making your message more compelling and memorable.

Rhetoric, the art of persuasion, plays a crucial role in enhancing your argument. Aristotle's rhetorical triangle—ethos, pathos, and logos—provides a framework for engaging your audience on multiple levels. Ethos appeals to credibility; establish your authority and trustworthiness by demonstrating knowledge and integrity. Pathos engages the emotions, using storytelling, vivid language, or personal anecdotes to connect with your audience on a human level. Logos is the logical appeal, relying on clear and rational arguments backed by evidence. Together, these elements create a well-rounded argument that resonates with diverse audiences. Rhetorical questions can also be a powerful tool, prompting your audience to actively reflect and engage with your message. By asking questions that lead to your desired conclusion, you guide your audience's thought process, making your argument more persuasive.

Consider the power of these techniques in action through examples of effective persuasive speeches. Political campaign speeches often masterfully blend ethos, pathos, and logos to rally support and inspire action. They present clear claims supported by logical reasoning and emotional appeals that resonate with the audience's values and aspirations. Motivational talks, like those given by leaders or coaches, use personal stories and vivid imagery to inspire change and encourage personal growth. They're crafted to evoke strong emotional responses, encouraging the audience to envision new possibilities. Meanwhile, a pitch that secured funding might use the problem-solution approach, presenting a pressing issue, demonstrating the urgency, and offering an innovative solution backed by compelling data.

Exercise: Analyzing a Persuasive Speech

Select a famous speech or TED Talk. As you watch or read, identify the speaker's claim, how they structure their argument, and their rhetorical techniques. Note examples of ethos, pathos, and logos. Reflect on how effectively the speaker engaged and persuaded their audience.

Persuasion is more than just convincing someone to see things your way; it's about creating a connection that aligns your message with their beliefs and values. Whether trying to influence a boardroom full of executives or inspiring a group of young leaders, mastering persuasive arguments will amplify your impact. As you refine these skills, visualize the potential doors they can open, from career advancements to new ventures and beyond.

Concluding with a Powerful Call to Action

As you stand before your audience, nearing the end of your presentation, the air is thick with anticipation. This is the moment to seal the deal, to transform your words from mere speech into a catalyst for action. The call to action (CTA) is where your message culminates, urging your audience to take the next step. It's not just a formality; it's the bridge between your ideas and real-world change. The purpose of a CTA is to inspire, motivate, and guide your audience toward a specific action. Whether it's adopting a new mindset, supporting a cause, or purchasing a product, a strong CTA leaves your audience with clarity and conviction about what comes next.

Developing a compelling call to action (CTA) demands thoughtful deliberation. Begin by making your CTA urgent and specific. Create a sense of immediacy with phrases like "Act now" or "Seize this opportunity," compelling your audience to move swiftly. Clarity in your request is equally vital; rather than broad suggestions, provide precise directions or steps. If advocating for donations, for instance, recommend a specific amount or method. If encouraging a new practice, detail the initial actions they should undertake. Emphasizing the key benefits also plays a crucial role. Remind your audience of the tangible value they gain by responding to your CTA, be it personal development, financial benefits, or contributing to a communal cause. By underscoring these advantages, you underscore the significance of their action.

The delivery of your call to action is as crucial as its content. Convey confidence and enthusiasm through a robust vocal delivery. Your tone should mirror the urgency and significance of your appeal, captivating your audience and reinforcing the call to act. Enhancing your CTA with visual elements can further bolster its impact. Employ slides, images, or videos that reinforce your message, providing a memorable visual cue to accompany your verbal prompt. This blend of auditory and visual stimuli crafts a more compelling and memorable CTA, ensuring your audience departs with a clear understanding of the steps ahead. Reflect on the impactful endings of renowned presentations. Inspirational speeches frequently culminate in a resonant call to action, leveraging transformational stories to motivate personal change. Similarly, effective sales pitches conclude with a persuasive invitation to invest, utilizing compelling evidence and testimonials to substantiate the call. These instances illustrate how a meticulously crafted CTA can motivate action and imprint a lasting impression, ensuring your message resonates well beyond the conclusion of your presentation.

A powerful CTA is your opportunity to leave a lasting impact, transform your words into action, and inspire your audience to make a change. By crafting an urgent, specific, and confident CTA, you can ensure your presentation ends on a high note, motivating your audience to take the steps you've outlined.

Building Rapport with Diverse Audiences

Imagine entering a room where every face is a unique tapestry of cultures, experiences, and perspectives. As a speaker, your goal is not just to share information but to connect and weave a thread of understanding and empathy through your words. This connection begins with a deep understanding of your audience's demographics. Knowing who they are—culturally, socially, and professionally—can significantly influence how you build rapport. Each audience comes with a distinct background that shapes their perceptions and expectations. By researching cultural norms, you gain insight into what resonates with them, what might offend them, and how best to engage their interest. This knowledge allows you to tailor your language and examples to align with their experiences, creating a personalized and relevant presentation. It's about speaking their language, not just literally but figuratively, tapping into what matters most to them.

Creating an inclusive environment is not just a strategy; it's necessary in today's diverse world. It starts with using inclusive language that acknowledges and respects every individual's identity and experience. Avoiding assumptions and generalizations is key, as is choosing words that make everyone feel seen and  valued. For example, addressing a group with "Hi everyone" instead of "Hi guys" is a small change that can make a big difference. Acknowledging diverse perspectives in your presentation also fosters inclusivity. Invite different viewpoints, encourage dialogue, and show appreciation for the varied experiences your audience brings. This approach enriches your presentation and makes your audience feel valued and respected.

Finding common ground is a powerful way to build rapport, as it bridges your experiences and those of your audience. Relating personal experiences to audience challenges can humanize you as a speaker, making you more relatable and approachable. You may have faced similar obstacles in your career or shared goals that align with theirs. Highlighting mutual goals or values can also foster connection. When your audience sees that you share their aspirations or concerns, they're more likely to engage with your message and see its relevance to their lives. This shared understanding can transform your presentation from a monologue into a meaningful dialogue.

Leaders who excel in building rapport often do so through authenticity and empathy. Former US president Barack Obama, for instance, is known for his use of humor and relatability. He often shares personal anecdotes and observations that resonate with his audience, breaking down barriers and creating a sense of camaraderie. His speeches are sprinkled with humor that disarms and engages, making complex issues more accessible. Similarly, Oprah

Winfrey's empathetic storytelling connects deeply with audiences. She shares her struggles and triumphs openly, inviting listeners to reflect on their experiences. Her ability to weave personal stories into broader narratives makes her messages powerful and impactful. These leaders demonstrate that building rapport is not about charisma alone; it's about being genuine, listening actively, and engaging with others on a human level.

Rapport is the foundation upon which effective communication is built. It's what turns a good presentation into a memorable one. By understanding your audience, creating an inclusive environment, and establishing common ground, you lay the groundwork for a meaningful connection. This connection enhances the impact of your message and enriches the experience for you and your audience. As you hone these skills, you'll find that building rapport becomes second nature, an integral part of your speaking repertoire. With each presentation, you strengthen your ability to communicate across diverse landscapes, preparing you for the challenges and opportunities that lie ahead.

As we conclude this chapter, remember that engaging and persuading your audience is about more than delivering a message—it's about fostering a connection that resonates. With these skills in hand, you're ready to move forward, exploring how to navigate questions and audience interaction in our next chapter.

Chapter 5

Navigating Questions and Audience Interaction

Imagine you're at the conclusion of your presentation, the room alive with curiosity, as hands shoot up and questions fill the air. This is where the real connection with your audience takes place—during the Q&A session. It's a moment that can transform a good presentation into a great one, showcasing your expertise and ability to engage directly with your audience's thoughts and concerns. But for many, this can also be a daunting part of public speaking. The key to navigating this successfully lies in thorough preparation, which can bolster your confidence and ensure smooth interactions.

Preparation for a Q&A session starts long before you step onto the stage. It's about anticipating your audience's questions and crafting concise, thoughtful responses. Begin by brainstorming potential questions, considering the angles from which your audience might approach your topic. Consider what aspects of your presentation might spark curiosity or require further clarification. Olivia Mitchell, in her work on Q&A preparation, emphasizes the importance of this step, particularly for those who might struggle with thinking on their feet. Collaborate with colleagues or friends with similar knowledge levels to your audience to simulate realistic questions. This exercise helps anticipate inquiries and uncovers areas of your presentation that may need reinforcing.

As you prepare your answers, focus on clarity and brevity. Acknowledge the underlying concerns behind each question, and aim to find common ground with your audience. This approach fosters a sense of understanding and respect, which can enhance the interaction. Practicing your responses out loud is crucial; it refines your delivery and reduces nervousness. This preparation mirrors rehearsing for the main presentation, allowing you to navigate the Q&A with confidence and poise.

Another vital aspect is structuring the Q&A session. Allocate a specific time at the end of your presentation for questions. This approach signals to your audience that their inquiries are valued and that you are open to dialogue. Setting clear guidelines for question submission can streamline the process, ensuring the session runs smoothly. Encourage your audience to jot down questions during your talk, which can be submitted to you or a team member at the designated time. This method helps manage the flow of questions and allows you to address them efficiently.

Technology can be a powerful ally in handling Q&A sessions in today's digital age. Tools like Slido offer platforms for real-time question submission, facilitating audience interaction without the chaos of overlapping voices. This tool allows participants to ask questions anonymously and vote on the most pressing ones. By integrating tools like Slido into your presentation, you create a dynamic and interactive experience that engages everyone, even those who might be hesitant to speak up. This technology enhances engagement and provides valuable analytics and feedback, helping you gauge audience interest and adjust future presentations accordingly.

Consider the example of a panel discussion, where Q&A sessions are structured yet fluid. Panelists often use a moderator to field questions, ensuring that each inquiry is addressed in an organized manner. The moderator might group similar questions or prioritize those that align with the session's objectives. This format keeps the conversation focused and allows for a deeper exploration of topics. Adopting similar strategies ensures that your Q&A session is not just a formality but a meaningful extension of your presentation.

Techniques for Managing Unexpected Questions

Imagine you're standing confidently at the end of your presentation, and suddenly, a question from the audience catches you off guard. It's a scenario every speaker faces at some point. Remaining composed when faced with unexpected questions is crucial. One effective method to maintain your cool is through controlled breathing. When anxiety strikes, your breath becomes your anchor. Take a slow, deep breath to calm your nerves. This simple yet powerful technique helps center your thoughts and clear your mind. It's like hitting the reset button, allowing you to approach the question with a fresh perspective. Remember, your composure reflects your professionalism.

But what if the question falls outside your expertise? It's perfectly okay not to have all the answers. Acknowledging this openly can actually build trust with your audience. Say something like, "That's a great question, and I want to give you the best answer possible. Let me find out more and get back to you." This shows integrity and willingness to learn. Alternatively, redirect the question to someone more knowledgeable, if applicable. For instance, if you're presenting with a team, you might say, "I think Jamie, our lead researcher, can provide more insight on that." This not only keeps the conversation going but also highlights your collaborative spirit.

Developing quick-thinking skills can also help you handle unexpected questions with ease. Practicing improvisation exercises can enhance your ability to think on your feet. These exercises encourage you to respond spontaneously, building confidence in handling whatever comes your way. Try engaging in activities that require you to make quick decisions or come up with creative solutions on the spot. Over time, these skills will transfer to your speaking engagements, helping you tackle unexpected questions effortlessly. It's about building mental agility, allowing you to navigate the unknown confidently.

Honesty and transparency are your allies when responding to questions. By admitting your knowledge gaps, you not only maintain credibility but also demonstrate humility. Audiences appreciate authenticity and can often sense when a speaker is trying to bluff their way through an answer. You foster a culture of openness and mutual respect by expressing a genuine willingness to learn. This honesty encourages your audience to engage more openly, knowing their questions are valued and taken seriously. In the world of public speaking, it's not just about having all the answers—it's about fostering an environment where everyone feels comfortable exploring ideas together.

Encouraging Audience Participation

Imagine standing in front of your audience, not as a lecturer, but as a facilitator of an engaging dialogue. Active participation can transform a presentation from a one-sided monologue into a dynamic exchange of ideas. When your audience is involved, their retention of the material increases significantly. Participation encourages them to process information actively, making it more memorable and impactful. This engagement enhances learning and fosters a sense of ownership over the content. Your audience becomes co-creators of the experience, and this shared journey enriches the learning process for everyone involved.

Consider incorporating open-ended questions into your presentation to prompt this kind of participation. These questions encourage dialogue by inviting your audience to share their thoughts and perspectives. Rather than asking yes-or-no questions, pose inquiries

that require more elaborate responses. For example, instead of asking, "Do you agree with this statement?" consider asking, "How do you see this concept applying to your current projects?" This approach opens the floor to diverse viewpoints and encourages deeper thinking and interaction.

Live polls are another effective strategy to gauge audience opinion and stimulate engagement. By implementing real-time polling, you can capture immediate feedback and adjust your presentation accordingly. These polls serve multiple purposes: they provide insight into the audience's standpoint on specific issues, highlight areas of consensus or divergence, and offer a moment of interaction that breaks the flow of a traditional presentation. Seeing the results unfold in real-time can also spark further discussion as participants react to the collective responses of their peers.

In today's digital age, interactive tools are invaluable for facilitating audience participation. Apps designed for real-time feedback can revolutionize how you engage with your audience. These platforms allow attendees to submit questions, participate in polls, and even generate word clouds that visualize collective ideas. The anonymity feature encourages even the most reserved individuals to contribute without fear of judgment. This technology seamlessly integrates into your presentation, creating a layer of interactivity that can transform the energy in the room.

Creating a participatory environment starts with setting a welcoming tone from the moment your presentation begins. Encourage your audience to share by creating a supportive atmosphere. Acknowledge contributions positively and address each participant with respect and appreciation. This approach fosters a culture of openness, where attendees feel comfortable expressing themselves. You might start by sharing a personal anecdote or humorous observation to break the ice, setting the stage for a relaxed and engaging session. This openness can lead to unexpected insights and enrich the overall experience as diverse voices contribute to the tapestry of the conversation.

Handling Difficult or Hostile Questions

Imagine you're in the middle of a vibrant presentation when, suddenly, a challenging question pierces the air. The atmosphere shifts slightly as all eyes turn to you, expecting a response. This is the moment where your skills as a speaker are truly tested. Handling difficult or hostile questions requires a calm and professional demeanor. It begins with active listening, a tool that allows you to acknowledge concerns genuinely. By focusing intently on the questioner, you show respect for their viewpoint, even if it's confrontational. This act of listening alone can diffuse tension, as it demonstrates your willingness to engage and understand. Responding with empathy further softens the interaction. Acknowledging the emotion behind the question—perhaps frustration or confusion—shows that you are not just hearing but genuinely listening. This empathy can transform a potentially hostile exchange into a constructive dialogue, as the questioner feels their concerns are validated.

Maintaining authority and respect while addressing difficult questions is crucial. Asserting yourself doesn't mean dominating the conversation; it's about setting boundaries politely. You might say, "I see where you're coming from; however, let's approach this from another angle." This approach keeps the conversation respectful and focused. Reframing hostile questions into constructive dialogue can also be highly effective. Turn a pointed question into a broader discussion point, inviting others to contribute. For example, in political debates, skilled speakers often redirect challenging questions to highlight their key messages, maintaining control of the narrative. By reframing, you manage the question and steer the conversation in a direction that aligns with your presentation's goals, showcasing your ability to handle pressure with poise.

Consider the use of humor as a strategic tool. A light, non-offensive joke can diffuse hostility and ease tension in tense moments. However, humor must be used carefully to avoid exacerbating the situation. The key is to ensure that your humor doesn't dismiss the question or belittle the questioner. Instead, aim for a light-hearted comment that acknowledges the question while gently steering the mood toward a more positive interaction. For instance, a speaker might respond to a particularly tough question with a smile and say, "Well, I see someone's been doing their homework!" This response acknowledges the challenge while lightening the atmosphere, paving the way for a more open and relaxed dialogue.

Diplomatic responses are your arsenal in managing hostility. Consider a political debate where a candidate faces a barrage of tough questions. Rather than becoming defensive, the candidate might respond with measured, thoughtful answers that address the concerns while reinforcing their stance. By maintaining composure and demonstrating respect, they showcase their leadership qualities and ability to handle pressure. This approach addresses the immediate concern and enhances credibility and respect among the audience.

Building Rapport Through Interactive Exercises

You've most likely experienced the difference between a presentation that merely informs and one that truly connects. This connection often stems from the rapport you build with your audience. Rapport isn't just about making a good impression; it's about creating a sense of trust and mutual understanding that can transform the atmosphere of the room. When you share experiences, even briefly, you establish a common ground. This shared space can make your audience more receptive, as they feel you're speaking with them, not at them. It's this bond that turns passive listeners into active participants, engaging more deeply with your message.

One effective way to build this connection is through interactive exercises. Icebreakers are a great start. They can dissolve the initial stiffness in a room, making people more comfortable and open. These activities don't have to be elaborate. A simple round of introductions with a twist—like sharing a fun fact or a personal goal—can break the ice. Such a small interaction sets a friendly tone and makes everyone feel a part of the group. Once the ice is broken, you can move into group discussions. These deeper interactions allow for the exchange of ideas and foster a sense of community. By dividing your audience into smaller groups and giving them a topic to discuss, you encourage them to engage with each other, providing diverse perspectives and enriching the conversation.

Adapting these exercises to suit your audience is crucial. A professional setting might call for more structured activities. Consider using case studies or problem-solving exercises that relate directly to their field. These activities build rapport and add value by enhancing their learning experience. In a more informal setting, you can afford to be playful. Incorporate games or storytelling rounds that encourage creativity and laughter. The key is to gauge your audience's comfort level and adjust accordingly. Tailoring your approach ensures everyone feels included and valued, regardless of the context.

Consider the impact of a successful interactive session. Imagine a workshop where participation is high, and energy is palpable. I recall attending a leadership seminar where the speaker used role-playing exercises. Participants were asked to step into different leadership roles and navigate hypothetical scenarios. This exercise broke the monotony and allowed us to apply theoretical concepts practically. The result was a room buzzing with insights and camaraderie. Such sessions leave a lasting impression, encouraging active learning and fostering connections beyond the presentation itself.

Using Feedback Loops to Enhance Engagement

Think of feedback loops as the pulse of your presentation's vitality. They're the channels through which you receive insights that can significantly boost your presentation quality and audience satisfaction. Feedback is not a one-time event; it's a cycle that, when embraced, leads to iterative improvement. Imagine each presentation as a stepping stone, with feedback guiding your path to becoming an even more effective communicator. It's not just about hearing what went well or what didn't; it's about continually integrating that information to refine your approach. Engaging in this ongoing process creates a dynamic learning environment where you and your audience grow.

Collecting feedback effectively requires a strategic approach. Online surveys are invaluable for post-event reflections, allowing participants to share their thoughts once they've had time to process your presentation. These surveys should be concise yet comprehensive, asking specific questions about the content, delivery, and overall experience. Real-time feedback tools can capture immediate reactions during the presentation itself. These tools provide a snapshot of the audience's engagement and allow you to adjust. Using these technologies creates a two-way dialogue that enhances the interactive experience, making your audience feel heard and valued.

Once you've gathered feedback, the real work begins: implementing it into your future presentations. Start by analyzing the feedback data to identify common themes or recurring suggestions. Such analysis is your roadmap, highlighting areas for improvement and affirming your strengths. Create an action plan that outlines specific changes or enhancements based on this feedback. For instance, if multiple attendees suggest more interactive elements, consider incorporating live polls or Q&A sessions into your next talk. The key is not to view feedback as criticism but as constructive guidance that propels your development as a speaker.

Integrating feedback effectively can lead to remarkable improvements in audience engagement. Consider a speaker who incorporated more pauses and interactive moments after receiving feedback about their presentation's pacing. The result was a noticeable increase in audience participation and satisfaction. This transformation showcases the power of feedback when applied thoughtfully. Another success story involves a presenter who used feedback about their slide design to simplify visuals, making their content more accessible and engaging. These examples highlight the benefits of listening to your audience and adapting accordingly.

Embracing feedback loops transcends mere presentation refinement; it cultivates an ethos of perpetual growth and partnership with your audience. Such an approach enhances your effectiveness as a speaker and enriches the overall experience for those who attend your talks. By valuing and implementing feedback, you demonstrate a commitment to excellence and a willingness to grow and evolve, qualities that resonate with any audience. Through feedback, you turn each presentation into a learning opportunity, ensuring your message reaches its full potential.

Make a Difference with Your Review

Unlock the Power of Generosity

> *"The best way to find yourself is to lose yourself in the service of others."*
>
> — *Mahatma Gandhi*

Public speaking is more than just words—it's about connecting, inspiring, and making a difference. If this book has helped you in any way, I have a small favor to ask.

Would you help someone just like you—eager to become a confident speaker but unsure where to begin?

My mission is to make public speaking easier, less scary, and even enjoyable for everyone. But to reach more people, I need your help.

Most people decide what to read based on reviews. That's why your thoughts matter. By leaving a quick review, you could help someone take their first step toward speaking with confidence. Your words might be the push they need to:

- Speak up in a meeting without fear.
- Nail an important presentation at work.
- Step onto a stage and share their story with the world.
- Finally conquer their fear of public speaking.

Leaving a review takes less than a minute, but its impact could last a lifetime.

To share your thoughts, scan the QR code below or visit:

[http://www.amazon.com/review/review-your-purchases/?asin=B0F9JQXPSD]

If you love helping others, you're my kind of person. Thank you from the bottom of my heart!

— Leanne Mauro

Chapter 6

Mastering Vocal Dynamics and Body Language

Exercises to Master Vocal Variety

Imagine listening to a speaker whose voice flows like a symphony, each note placed perfectly to stir emotions, emphasize key points, and hold your attention. This isn't just good fortune but the result of mastering vocal variety. When you think about what makes a speech memorable, it often comes down to how it's delivered, not just what's being said. Vocal variety is the art of using pitch, tone, and pace to breathe life into your words. It keeps your audience engaged, helping them follow your narrative and feel every emotion you intend to convey. Without this, even the most compelling content can fall flat.

Let's start with pitch. Think of it as the melody of your speech. By adjusting the pitch, you can convey a wide range of emotions. A higher pitch might express excitement or urgency, while a lower pitch can add gravity or calmness. This modulation can help highlight important information, drawing your audience's focus exactly where you want it. Exercises like pitch glides, where you move your voice smoothly from low to high and back, can help you gain control over your pitch. Regular practice of pitch exercises will give you the flexibility to express yourself fully and keep your delivery dynamic.

Tone is another critical element, shaping how your message is perceived. Tone is the color of your voice; it affects how your audience interprets your words. A warm, friendly tone can make your audience feel welcomed and included, while a more serious tone might underscore the importance of your message. The key is to match your tone to your message and context. Consider the emotional weight of your content and the mood you wish to create. This alignment ensures that your words and emotions resonate authentically, enhancing your connection with the audience.

Pace is the speed at which you speak. It dramatically influences audience understanding and engagement. A deliberate, slower pace allows your audience to absorb complex information, while a quicker pace can inject energy and excitement. Think of pacing like a conductor leading an orchestra, guiding the tempo to match the piece's mood. Techniques such as consciously slowing down for emphasis or speeding up to build momentum can enhance your speech's impact. Practicing these strategies will help you manage your speech's flow, ensuring your audience remains captivated.

Exercise: Pitch Gliding

1. Choose a comfortable starting pitch (e.g., mid-range note)
2. Take a deep diaphragmatic breath to support your voice.
3. Using an "ooh" (as in "food") or "ee" (as in "see") sound, smoothly slide your pitch from low to high.
4. Imagine your voice moving like an elevator or siren, ascending smoothly.
5. Avoid breaking or straining—keep the transition seamless. With continual practice, you will be able to pass through any breaks in your voice you may have. Be gentle with yourself.

6. Once you reach a comfortable high note, glide back down to your starting pitch.
7. Maintain breath support and relaxation to avoid cracking.

Tip: Perform this exercise for around 2 minutes daily to develop smooth pitch transitions and vocal flexibility.

To expand your range, repeat the exercise, starting slightly lower or higher each time.

- Experiment with different vowel sounds like "ah" or "ng" for variation.

Exercise: Vocal Variety Practice

1. Choose a Passage: Select a paragraph from a favorite book or speech.
2. Experiment with Pitch: Read it aloud, varying your pitch for different emotions.
3. Adjust Your Tone: Practice delivering the same passage with warm, earnest, and enthusiastic tones.
4. Play with Pace: Experiment with different speeds, noting how each affects the passage's impact.
5. Record and Reflect: Listen to your practice to identify strengths and areas for improvement.

Mastering vocal variety transforms your speech from mere words into an experience, captivating and persuading your audience in ways that linger long after you've finished speaking.

Exercises for Improving Vocal Clarity

Picture a speaker whose words flow effortlessly, each syllable crisp and clear, leaving no room for misunderstanding. This clarity is the cornerstone of effective communication, ensuring your message is heard and understood. When you speak clearly, you project confidence and professionalism, qualities that captivate your audience and foster trust. Enunciation, the careful articulation of sounds, plays a crucial role here. It's not just about avoiding mumbling; it's about ensuring each word is delivered with precision. This level of clarity can transform a simple message into something compelling.

Vocal exercises are essential to create a commanding voice that delivers a compelling message. Tongue twisters, though playful, are powerful tools for improving articulation. They challenge your pronunciation and dexterity, forcing you to focus on each sound. Try classics like "Peter Piper picked a peck of pickled peppers" to warm up your vocal cords. Breathing exercises also support vocal strength, connecting you to your full voice. Diaphragmatic breathing, where you breathe deeply from your diaphragm, not only enhances control and stability, providing a strong foundation for your voice, but also connects you to your power center, producing a full, rich, commanding voice. It not only aids clarity but also boosts your overall vocal presence. Incorporating these exercises into your routine can gradually improve your speech clarity, making your delivery more engaging and effective.

Consistency is key to developing vocal clarity. Establish a daily warm-up routine to ensure your voice is always at its best. Begin with gentle exercises, like humming, to relax your vocal cords, gradually increasing intensity as you progress. Regular practice will help you maintain clarity even when speaking for extended periods. It's not just about the exercises themselves but about the discipline of consistently doing them. Over time, this commitment will yield noticeable improvements, allowing you to speak confidently in any situation.

Common clarity issues, like mumbling, often stem from a lack of awareness or nervousness. Overcoming these requires conscious effort. Practice speaking slowly and deliberately, focusing on each word's enunciation. Visualization can help—imagine your voice reaching the farthest corners of the room, each word landing with precision. Recording yourself and listening critically can also identify areas for improvement. By addressing these issues head-on, you can refine your delivery and ensure your message is communicated with the clarity and impact it deserves.

Power Voice Warm-Up

1. **Observe your Breath:** Start by simply observing your breath for a minute or so. Please don't change it. Just observe it. Are you breathing in a shallow and restricted manner, or are you breathing calmly down into your belly? Observe and accept.
2. **Humming:** Humming is one of the safest ways to warm up your voice. Slowly start breathing down into your diaphragm. When ready, hum into different parts of your body, like your chest, cheekbones, belly, legs, and arms. Don't be afraid to get into your body and move around.
3. **Lip Trills:** Take a breath into your diaphragm and let the air out through softly closed lips. Once you've done this a few times on the same sound, repeat, but this time, you can move up and down the scale. Don't force this; only go to comfortable highs and lows. Your range will expand as you keep practicing.
4. **Tongue Trills:** As above, take in a diaphragmatic breath, but this time, place the tip of your tongue behind your top teeth and release the air via a tongue trill. This may be tricky at first, but keep practicing, and you will get it. Again, start on the one note, and with each repeated cycle, trill up and down your scale, ensuring you don't force your range.

Only go as far as comfortable. Practicing this exercise will expand your range over time.
5. **Classic Tongue Twisters:** Try these tongue twisters. Repeat each one 3-5 times, seeing how fast and precise you can make them.

- "She sells seashells by the seashore."
- "Peter Piper picked a peck of pickled peppers."
- "How much wood would a woodchuck chuck if a woodchuck could chuck wood?"
- "Red leather, yellow leather."
- "Betty Botter bought some butter, but she said the butter's bitter."

The Power of Pause: Using Silence Effectively

Imagine you're listening to a speaker who seems to command the room, not just with their words, but with their use of silence. This isn't a coincidence. Pauses are a powerful tool in public speaking, and when used strategically, they can emphasize key points and give the audience space to process information. Pauses for dramatic effect can turn a simple statement into a profound moment. They allow your words to sink in, giving your audience time to reflect on what you've said. A well-timed pause can be more impactful than the words themselves, creating a sense of anticipation and focus that grips attention.

There are different types of pauses, each serving a purpose. Planned pauses are deliberate and used to emphasize a point or allow your audience to absorb complex information. They can be inserted before revealing a key insight, heightening the drama and ensuring your message lands with impact. On the other hand, spontaneous pauses happen naturally during speech, often as you collect your thoughts or respond to audience reactions. Learning to implement these strategic pauses involves practice and awareness. It means knowing your speech well enough to identify moments where silence will add value, whether before a key revelation or during a transition between segments.

Timing and placement of pauses are crucial. Placing a pause before a significant point can build anticipation, making your audience lean in, eager to hear what comes next. Use pauses to transition between segments, allowing your audience a moment to catch up and prepare for the next part of your message. This not only aids understanding but also maintains engagement, as it prevents your speech from feeling rushed or overwhelming. The psychological impact of silence is profound. It creates a space where anticipation builds, focus sharpens, and your audience becomes more receptive to your message. Silence can be a speaker's secret weapon, used wisely to enhance delivery and captivate an audience. Mastering the pause adds depth to your speech, transforming your delivery from ordinary to extraordinary.

Eliminate Filler Words for Clear Impactful Speech

We've all been there—standing in front of an audience, searching for words, and before we know it, "um," "uh," "like," or "you know" slips out. Filler words are those little verbal hiccups that serve as placeholders when our brains are catching up to our mouths. They often creep in when we're unsure or need a moment to think. While seemingly harmless, these fillers can undermine your authority and distract from your message. In professional settings, they can dilute the impact of your speech, making you appear less confident or prepared. It's crucial to be aware of these habits and work on minimizing them to maintain your credibility.

Eliminating fillers is about more than just polishing your speech—it's about enhancing your presence. When you speak without fillers, your words carry more weight. Your audience focuses on your message, not on the interruptions. To overcome this habit, start by identifying your common fillers. Record a practice session and listen carefully.

Note the words you use most frequently as crutches. Awareness is the first step to change. Once you know your patterns, you can begin to replace fillers with pauses. Silence, strategically used, allows you to gather your thoughts without verbal clutter, adding a touch of professionalism to your delivery.

Slow down your speech. Rushing often leads to fillers as your brain races to keep up. Slowing down gives yourself time to think and choose your words deliberately. Practice speaking at a measured pace, focusing on clarity and intention. Visualization techniques can also help. Picture yourself speaking smoothly and confidently, with each word landing precisely. This mental rehearsal can reinforce positive speech habits. Thorough preparation reduces the need for fillers. Knowing your material inside and out makes you less likely to stumble over your words. Rehearse until the content feels natural, allowing you to present with ease.

Remember that staying relaxed under pressure is key. Anxiety often fuels the use of fillers. Incorporate relaxation techniques, like box breathing or visualization, into your routine. This practice can calm your nerves and enhance your focus. A confident speaker commands attention and respect, and by minimizing fillers, you ensure your audience hears your message loud and clear.

Body Language Essentials for Speakers

Picture yourself standing before a crowd, ready to deliver your message. While your words are crucial, your body language speaks volumes, often louder than your voice. Every movement, from a slight hand gesture to a confident stance, can either reinforce or contradict what you're saying. When body language aligns with your message, it boosts credibility, making your audience more likely to trust and engage with you. Conversely, mixed signals can create doubt and confusion. Your audience reads your non-verbal cues instinctively, and these cues shape their perception of you as a speaker.

To convey confidence and openness, your posture should be upright yet relaxed. Imagine a string gently pulling you upward from the crown of your head, elongating your spine. This posture not only exudes confidence but also makes breathing easier, supporting vocal delivery. Eye contact is another powerful tool. It connects you to your audience, making each person feel acknowledged. Pairing this with purposeful gestures makes your message even more compelling. Gestures should complement your words, not distract from them. For instance, open palms can suggest honesty and openness, while pointing can emphasize a particular point.

It's easy to fall into negative body language habits, especially under pressure. Crossing your arms might feel protective, but it can signal defensiveness, closed-mindedness or insecurity. Similarly, fidgeting can indicate nervousness, diverting attention from your message. Be mindful of these pitfalls. Practicing in front of a mirror or recording yourself can help you identify and correct these habits, cultivating a more confident and engaging presence.

Cultural nuances add another layer of complexity to body language. Gestures and acceptable expressions in one culture might be offensive or confusing in another. For example, maintaining eye contact is seen as respectful in many Western cultures, while in some Asian cultures, it might be perceived as confrontational. Being aware of these differences is crucial when addressing diverse audiences. Adapting your body language to be culturally sensitive shows respect and enhances understanding, allowing your message to resonate more effectively across cultural boundaries. Recognizing these nuances ensures you communicate effectively and inclusively, reaching your audience meaningfully.

Enhancing Stage Presence Through Movement

Stage presence is that intangible quality that draws all eyes to you when you speak. It's not only about confidence but also how effectively you use movement to engage your audience and assert authority. Imagine a speaker who stands stiffly in one spot; their words may be powerful, but the delivery can feel static and uninspiring. Effective movement, on the other hand, captivates. It adds a dynamic element to your presentation, making your message more memorable. When you move purposefully, you help your audience focus on your key points, guiding their attention and reinforcing your message through physical cues.

Using space strategically can transform your stage presence. Think of the stage as your canvas and your movement as the brushstrokes that paint your message. To use space effectively, start by positioning yourself to connect with the audience. Move closer to them for intimacy or to emphasize a point, and step back to reset their focus or introduce a new idea. Spatial awareness creates a rhythm that can make your presentation more engaging. Movement should be purposeful; every step should have a reason. For instance, transitioning from one part of the stage to another can signify a shift in topic or tone, keeping your audience visually and mentally engaged.

Equally important is knowing when to stand still. Stillness can be just as powerful as movement. It anchors your message, drawing your audience's attention to your words. When delivering a critical point, pausing movement can emphasize the gravity of your message. This balance between movement and stillness adds a layer of sophistication to your delivery. It helps you control the pace and flow of your presentation, ensuring that your audience remains attentive and engaged.

To develop this skill, practice is essential. Begin by rehearsing in front of a mirror, paying close attention to your movements. Notice how they align with your speech, and adjust to ensure each movement complements your message. Consider filming yourself to gain a different perspective, watching for distracting habits or movements that might detract from your delivery. Through practice, you'll gain the confidence to move naturally and purposefully, enhancing your stage presence and making your presentations more impactful. As you refine this skill, you'll find that the stage becomes an extension of your message, amplifying your words and leaving a lasting impression on your audience.

The Role of Facial Expressions in Communication

Imagine delivering a speech where your words are perfectly synchronized with the emotions on your face, creating a harmony that captivates your audience. Facial expressions are a powerful tool in communication, conveying emotions and adding depth to your spoken words. They can underscore sincerity, highlight enthusiasm, and even express doubt without uttering a single word. This connection between facial expressions and audience engagement is profound; when your face reflects your message, it reinforces what you're saying, making it more believable and impactful. A simple smile can warm a room, while a furrowed brow might convey seriousness or concern, drawing your audience deeper into your narrative.

To use facial expressions effectively, consider them an extension of your storytelling. They should align with the emotions you wish to convey, enhancing clarity and making your message more relatable. Exercises to develop an expressive range can be as simple as practicing in front of a mirror. Observe your face and how it changes with different emotions. Try conveying a story using only your expressions, then add words and see how they complement each other. Practicing congruence between words and expressions ensures authenticity, as mismatched cues can create confusion or distrust. The goal is to make your expressions a natural accompaniment to your speech, seamlessly blending with your message.

Micro-expressions, those fleeting facial expressions that reveal genuine emotions, play a subtle yet significant role in communication. They can convey authenticity and sincerity, even if only visible for a fraction of a second. Recognizing and utilizing these micro-expressions can enhance your connection with the audience. Practice identifying these small cues in your expressions and those of others, as they often hold the truth of one's feelings. By becoming attuned to these nuances, you can ensure your expressions are consistent with your message, reinforcing trust and engagement.

Cultural differences can influence how facial expressions are perceived. In some cultures, a smile may signify agreement; in others, it might simply be polite acknowledgment. Awareness of these cultural contexts is crucial, especially when addressing diverse audiences. Adapt your expressions to ensure they resonate appropriately with your audience's cultural background, demonstrating respect and understanding. This sensitivity enhances your message and builds rapport, making your communication more effective and inclusive. Understanding these layers adds depth to your interactions, ensuring your expressions communicate as clearly as your words.

Chapter 7

Authenticity and Personal Branding

Imagine a crowded room where everyone is trying to speak louder than the next, vying for attention. Yet amid this cacophony, one voice doesn't try to shout—rather, it speaks with a quiet assurance that draws people in. This is the power of authenticity. In public speaking, authenticity is not just a nice-to-have; it's essential for true connection. It's about using your true voice —an expression of who you genuinely are. But what does it mean to find this voice? It's a journey of distinguishing between the natural voice you were born with and the speaking habits you've acquired over time. Your authentic voice is the one that resonates with your core values and beliefs, free from the layers of performance or pretense.

When you embrace your authentic voice, your communication becomes more impactful and genuine. It's the difference between reading from a script and speaking from the heart. An authentic voice isn't perfect, but it's real. It allows your personality to shine through, creating a genuine connection with your audience. As emphasized by American speaker Diane DiResta, this authenticity is valued because it aligns your words, voice, and actions with who you truly are. The challenge lies in peeling back the layers of learned habits to uncover that authentic voice. Exercises like journaling can be incredibly revealing. Take time to reflect on your speaking experiences, jotting down when you felt most comfortable and when you felt like you were putting on a facade. This practice helps you identify patterns and traits that define your authentic self.

Another way to uncover your unique voice is by seeking feedback from trusted friends or mentors. They can provide insights into how you come across and what feels genuine to them. Practicing in a safe environment allows you to experiment with different styles and approaches, gradually honing in on what feels most natural. Remember, feedback is a gift, offering perspectives you might not see yourself. The more you practice, the more your authentic voice will emerge. This process isn't about striving for perfection but embracing imperfections. Authenticity thrives on vulnerability and honesty. By sharing personal stories, including your struggles and triumphs, you invite your audience into your world, fostering trust and engagement.

You allow your humanity to shine through when you let go of perfection. Audiences connect with speakers who are real, not flawless. This connection builds trust, as listeners are likelier to relate to someone who acknowledges their imperfections. Authenticity in public speaking is not about putting on a show; it's about being yourself and letting that be enough. It's about speaking from the heart, which, in turn, enhances your presence and impact. Your authenticity is your greatest asset, setting you apart in a world that often values conformity.

Action Step: Spend some time journalling, reflecting on past speaking experiences. When did you feel most comfortable and authentic? When did you feel like you were putting on a facade?

On stage, demonstrating authenticity begins with openness. Maintain eye contact to forge a connection, letting your audience see that you're present with them in the moment. This simple act signals honesty and invites engagement. Share your personal motivations and aspirations, allowing your audience to understand your "why." This transparency turns a monologue into a dialogue, where listeners feel involved and invested in your message. Authenticity also means being comfortable with vulnerability. Sharing your journey, including the bumps along the way, can resonate deeply with your audience, showing them that you're relatable and trustworthy.

In practice, authentic communication has been the hallmark of many successful public figures. Consider Malala Yousafzai, whose speeches resonate with authenticity and sincerity. She speaks from her heart, sharing personal experiences and a vision for change. Her openness and genuine dedication to her cause have inspired millions, earning her trust and admiration worldwide. Authenticity in her communication makes her message powerful and memorable, serving as a testament to the impact of genuine connection.

Building a Personal Brand Through Public Speaking

In today's competitive world, a strong personal brand can be your greatest asset, especially in speaking engagements. Imagine this: you're preparing for a big presentation, and the audience already knows you—not just your name, but your values, your style, and what you stand for. This recognition comes from a well-crafted personal brand. It's what sets you apart, making you more than just another voice in the room. Your brand reflects who you are and what makes you unique as a speaker. It's a combination of your core values, your strengths, and those unique selling points that only you can offer. These elements combine to form a personal brand statement—a concise declaration of your identity and purpose as a speaker.

Identifying these key brand elements requires introspection. Start by defining your core values—what principles guide you personally and professionally? Consider your strengths, those talents and skills that come naturally to you. What makes you stand out in a crowd? These insights will help you craft your personal brand statement, a beacon guiding your speaking engagements. Alongside this, identify your signature speaking topics. What subjects ignite your passion and align with your expertise? When you speak on these topics, your enthusiasm and knowledge shine, reinforcing your brand.

Consistency is crucial in maintaining a cohesive personal brand. Your messaging should align across all platforms, whether a keynote speech, a social media post, or a blog article. This uniformity reinforces your identity and ensures your audience knows what to expect from you. Think of your brand as a promise—every interaction should reflect this promise, building trust and reliability. Consistent messaging doesn't mean repeating the same words but adhering to the same values and tone. It means speaking with the same voice, whether online or in person, creating a seamless experience for your audience.

Public speaking is a powerful tool for brand building. Each engagement enhances your visibility and credibility, positioning you as an expert in your field. Speaking events offer invaluable networking opportunities, allowing you to connect with industry leaders, potential clients, and like-minded individuals. These connections can lead to new opportunities and collaborations, further strengthening your brand. By leveraging public speaking, you amplify your reach, ensuring your message resonates with a broader audience. This visibility is not just about being seen; it's about being remembered.

Aligning Your Message with Core Values

Think of your message as a reflection of who you are, anchored in the values that define you. Value alignment in messaging is not just a concept; it's a powerful tool that enhances authenticity and impact. When your words mirror your core beliefs, your audience senses the sincerity in your delivery. This alignment creates a resonance that can be felt, fostering trust and engagement. First, identify personal and professional values that matter most to you. These could be integrity, innovation, empathy, or perseverance—whatever guides your decisions and actions. By understanding what you stand for, you can ensure that every speech you deliver is rooted in these principles, making your communication more compelling.

Crafting value-driven messages involves weaving these core values into your speech content and delivery. It's not about inserting values into your speech as an afterthought but integrating them seamlessly so they shape the narrative. Consider how Martin Luther King Jr.'s speeches centered around equality and justice, using value-based language to articulate a vision of a better future. Such speeches are memorable because of their eloquence and because they resonate deeply with fundamental human values. When you use language reflecting your values, clarity emerges, and your message strengthens. Your values become the lens through which your audience views your message, adding depth and meaning to your words.

Consistency in value alignment is crucial across all your interactions. It's about being true to your values when you speak and in every facet of your communication. Conduct regular value audits to ensure your actions and messages consistently reflect your core beliefs. This means evaluating your speeches, presentations, and even casual conversations to check for alignment. It's a practice that keeps you grounded and authentic, reinforcing your credibility and reliability. When your audience sees that your values guide every aspect of your communication, trust builds, and your influence grows.

Leaders renowned for their value alignment serve as powerful examples. Take Nelson Mandela, whose speeches consistently echoed his dedication to freedom and reconciliation. His unwavering commitment to these values inspired millions and left a lasting legacy. By analyzing how influential figures like Mandela use their values to guide their communication, you can gain insights into crafting resonating messages. Their speeches are not just words; they're manifestations of their deepest beliefs, delivered with a conviction that captivates and motivates. In emulating this approach, you can transform your communication into a force that informs and inspires.

Overcoming Imposter Syndrome with Cognitive Restructuring

Imposter syndrome is a sneaky adversary, one that quietly undermines your confidence and makes you question your worthiness to speak publicly. It's that inner voice whispering doubts, convincing you that you're a fraud waiting to be exposed. This psychological pattern is all too common among speakers, manifesting as anxiety and self-doubt. You might feel that your achievements are merely luck or that you don't deserve the platform you've earned. These feelings stem from cognitive distortions—skewed perceptions that distort reality. Recognizing these distortions, such as all-or-nothing thinking or catastrophizing, is the first step in dismantling imposter syndrome's grip. By identifying these thought patterns, you can begin to see them for what they are: barriers to your full potential.

Cognitive restructuring offers a way to challenge and change these negative thought patterns. This technique involves reframing your internal dialogue, turning self-doubt into self-assurance. Start by identifying those cognitive distortions that feed your imposter syndrome. Are you assuming that one mistake will ruin your entire speech? This all-or-nothing thinking can be countered with a more balanced view. Consider thought reframing exercises as a tool to reshape your mindset. When you catch yourself in negative self-talk, pause and reframe. Replace "I'm not good enough" with "I am prepared and capable." These small shifts in perspective can gradually build a more confident narrative.

Seeking external validation is another powerful way to combat imposter syndrome. Feedback from mentors and peers can provide an objective perspective on your capabilities, reinforcing your self-worth. Constructive feedback from trusted sources helps build self-assurance, offering insights you might overlook.  Requesting this feedback shows strength, not weakness, and signals your readiness to grow. When you hear from others that your message resonates, it becomes harder to doubt your abilities. They see your strengths that you might miss, and their encouragement can bolster your confidence.

Reframing negative thoughts involves more than just positive affirmations; it's about shifting your entire mindset. Cognitive techniques like visualization can help you see yourself succeeding, reinforcing positive beliefs. When self-critical thoughts arise, challenge them with evidence of your accomplishments. Use positive affirmations to replace limiting beliefs with empowering ones. This practice isn't just about ignoring negativity but acknowledging it and choosing a different narrative. Over time, these strategies help transform your internal dialogue, allowing you to stand confidently before any audience, assured of your worth and capability.

Action Steps to Overcome Imposter Syndrome:

- Replace self-doubt with affirmations, for example, "I am prepared and have something valuable to offer".
- Visualise: Close your eyes and picture yourself delivering your speech smoothly, making eye contact, and receiving

applause. Your brain will believe what it repeatedly imagines!
- Prepare & Practice: The more prepared and practiced you are, the more confident you will feel.
- Focus on your audience, not yourself.
- Embrace wins, no matter how small they seem.
- Keep Going!! The more you speak publicly, the more comfortable you'll become.

Cultivating Emotional Intelligence as a Speaker

Emotional intelligence stands as a cornerstone in the realm of impactful public speaking. It encapsulates the ability to discern, navigate, and leverage both your own emotions and those of your audience to enhance communication. For speakers, this skill is pivotal, enabling a deeper and more meaningful connection with the listeners. Central to emotional intelligence are self-awareness and empathy. Self-awareness allows you to acknowledge and understand your emotional state, influencing both your presentation and its reception. Empathy, conversely, equips you to perceive and react to the emotional signals of your audience, fostering an interactive and captivating dialogue. Identifying when your audience is captivated or when their attention drifts can transform a good presentation into an unforgettable one.

Developing emotional intelligence is not an overnight task, but with practice, it significantly enhances your speaking prowess. Start by incorporating mindfulness exercises into your daily routine. Mindfulness helps you become aware of your emotions in the present moment, allowing you to regulate them more effectively during your speeches. Emotional regulation exercises, such as deep breathing and visualization, can help maintain calm and clarity even in high-pressure situations. Additionally, engage in empathy-building activities, such as active listening exercises, where you put your focus entirely on understanding other people's perspectives. These practices improve your emotional awareness and equip you with the tools to connect more authentically with your audience.

The benefits of emotional intelligence in communication are profound. It leads to more empathetic interactions, fostering stronger rapport with your audience. You create an environment of mutual respect and understanding when you respond to their cues, whether nodding in agreement or showing concern. This rapport makes your audience more receptive to your message and more willing to engage with your ideas—moreover, emotional intelligence aids in gracefully handling audience feedback and questions. By remaining open and composed, even when faced with challenging inquiries, you demonstrate respect and attentiveness, which can diffuse tension and build trust.

- Consider speakers like the Dalai Lama, whose compassion and understanding resonate deeply with audiences worldwide. His ability to connect emotionally with people from all walks of life exemplifies the power of emotional intelligence. Similarly, Michelle Obama's storytelling often incorporates relatable experiences and emotions, making her speeches engaging and impactful. These speakers use emotional intelligence to bridge gaps, foster empathy, and create memorable experiences for their audiences, illustrating the profound impact of understanding and managing emotions in public speaking.

In this chapter, we have explored how to bring your authenticity to your speaking and how to continue to create trusting relationships with your audience. Now, let's move on to some gender-specific communication strategies.

Chapter 8

Gender-Specific Communication Strategies

Societal norms have historically influenced how men and women communicate. For centuries, women faced significant barriers in public discourse, often relegated to the background despite possessing valuable insights. Meanwhile, men frequently dominated the stage, shaping the narrative and setting the tone. This division has carved distinct paths in communication styles that still influence how we perceive speakers today.

Over time, these historical roles have evolved, but gender-specific traits remain evident in how individuals approach communication. Men often favor directness, a style that conveys authority and decisiveness. It's a trait that aligns with traditional masculine ideals of strength and independence. In contrast, women typically lean towards indirect communication, emphasizing collaboration and understanding. This approach resonates with the societal expectation of women as nurturers and consensus builders. These differences are not just surface deep; they reflect more profound cultural and psychological influences shaping how we express ourselves and how others perceive us.

In public speaking, these styles can lead to varied audience perceptions. Directness in men is often interpreted as confidence, whereas the same trait in women might be misread as aggression. Conversely, while celebrated for warmth, a woman's empathetic approach can sometimes be dismissed as a lack of authority. Such biases highlight the challenges of navigating gendered expectations in communication. Understanding these perceptions allows speakers to tailor their approach, ensuring their message is received as intended.

Balancing these gender-specific traits involves adopting complementary strategies. Male speakers can enhance their direct style by incorporating empathy, ensuring their message resonates emotionally. This can be achieved by sharing personal anecdotes or acknowledging the audience's feelings. Female speakers might balance their natural expressiveness with assertiveness, using clear, concise language to reinforce their authority. Practicing adaptable speaking techniques can help in this regard. Engaging in exercises such as role-playing different scenarios allows speakers to experiment with various styles and find an authentic yet effective balance.

Exercise: Exploring Your Communication Style

Reflect on your recent speaking experiences. Consider the following:

- Directness vs. Indirectness: Do you tend to be more direct or indirect in your communication? How does this affect your audience's perception?
- Emotional Expression: How do you convey emotions in your speech? Are there moments where different expressions enhance your message?
- Adaptability: Practice delivering a short speech using both direct and indirect styles. Note the differences in tone, impact, and audience engagement.

Understanding and adapting your communication style to suit your audience while staying true to yourself is key in public speaking. Recognizing the gender dynamics at play can empower you to navigate them with confidence and skill, ensuring your message is powerful and authentic.

Empowering Female Voices: Overcoming Stereotypes

Imagine a room full of eager listeners waiting to hear your insights. As you step up to speak, you're not just presenting your ideas; you're also navigating a landscape riddled with expectations. For many female speakers, this means confronting stereotypes that can overshadow their message. One prevalent stereotype is the perception of emotionality. Women are often unfairly characterized as being overly emotional, which can undermine their authority in the eyes of some audiences. This stereotype diminishes the power of authentic expression, turning a strength into a perceived weakness. Similarly, when women adopt assertive tones to convey their points, they're sometimes misidentified as aggressive rather than confident. This misperception can discourage women from speaking with the conviction that their male counterparts might exhibit without judgment.

To break free from these constraints, female speakers can employ several strategies. Confidence-building workshops are a great way to start. These workshops focus on enhancing self-assurance and providing tools to project confidence even when facing a skeptical audience. Women can learn to own their space and voice without apology by participating in these sessions. Additionally, role-playing assertive communication scenarios offers practical experience in handling difficult interactions. This technique allows women to practice delivering messages with clarity and authority, reinforcing the idea that assertiveness is a valuable communication tool, not a liability. Through role-playing, they can simulate real-world challenges, refining their responses and building resilience.

Success stories abound of women who have transcended these stereotypes to become powerful communicators. Sheryl Sandberg, former COO of Facebook, has become a beacon of leadership and inclusion. She champions women in the workplace, urging them to lean in and embrace leadership roles. Her talks are a testament to the effectiveness of combining empathy with assertiveness, challenging the status quo in male-dominated industries. Similarly, Malala Yousafzai's advocacy for girls' education showcases the strength of a voice that refuses to be silenced. Despite facing immense adversity, Malala's speeches resonate worldwide, demonstrating the power of speaking with both passion and purpose.

Embracing unique communication strengths is key to empowerment. Women naturally excel in empathy and relational skills, creating connections that deepen audience engagement. By leveraging these skills, female speakers can foster environments of openness and trust where their messages are heard and felt. Developing a personal speaking style incorporating these innate abilities can further enhance effectiveness. It's about finding an authentic balance, allowing women to speak with sincerity and impact. When women embrace their unique voices and communicate with confidence, they pave the way for others, reshaping the narrative and challenging stereotypes that have long limited their expression.

Leveraging Male Strengths: Authenticity and Authority

Imagine stepping onto a stage where your presence alone commands attention. This strength is often associated with male speakers—a commanding presence, conveying authority and confidence. Such a presence is not merely about physical stature or vocal volume; it's an energy that fills the room, compelling others to listen. This ability to assert dominance through presence and direct communication is typically rooted in traditional male roles, where clarity and decisiveness are prized. Men often excel in delivering messages with authority, using direct language that leaves little room for ambiguity. This style is particularly effective in environments that value straightforwardness and quick decision-making.

However, authority isn't just about being direct. Authenticity plays a crucial role, and storytelling is one of the most effective ways to achieve this. When you tell a story, you're not just sharing information; you're opening a window into your experiences. Authentic storytelling allows male speakers to connect on a personal level, humanizing their authority and making their message relatable. Balancing this authority with approachability can be a powerful combination. It involves speaking with conviction while remaining open to dialogue, ensuring your audience feels heard and valued. Practicing this balance can transform a speech from a monologue into a conversation, fostering engagement and trust.

Consider author and inspirational speaker on business leadership Simon Sinek's leadership presentations. They are a masterclass in direct yet empathetic communication. Sinek's approach combines clear, authoritative insights with stories that illustrate his points, inviting audiences to reflect and engage. This example highlights how male speakers can leverage their natural strengths while embracing authenticity and vulnerability.

Vulnerability in communication might seem counterintuitive to traditional notions of male strength, yet it is incredibly powerful. Embracing vulnerability means sharing personal stories that reveal not just successes but also challenges and failures. It's about showing that you, too, face obstacles and uncertainties. This openness can foster a deeper connection with your audience, as they see you not just as a speaker but as a fellow human being. Expressing empathy and understanding further enhances this connection, allowing you to build rapport and trust. By acknowledging your vulnerabilities, you invite your audience to do the same, creating a space where genuine dialogue can flourish.

Gender-Inclusive Language: Reaching a Broader Audience

Imagine speaking to a room filled with diverse individuals, each bringing their unique perspectives. In this scenario, your words have the power to connect or alienate. Gender-inclusive language is a key factor in ensuring your message reaches everyone effectively. Avoiding gendered assumptions creates an environment where all feel acknowledged and respected. This approach isn't simply about political correctness; it's about promoting equality and inclusivity. Language shapes perception, and using neutral pronouns and terms can dismantle barriers that might otherwise exclude certain individuals. It fosters a sense of belonging, which is crucial for effective communication in today's interconnected world. Using gender-inclusive language allows you to reach a wider audience, bridging gaps and fostering understanding across different backgrounds and identities.

To incorporate gender inclusivity into your speech and writing, start by replacing gender-specific terms with neutral alternatives. Instead of addressing a group as "guys," opt for "everyone", "all of you" or "team". These minor adjustments can significantly impact how your message is received. It's also vital to acknowledge diverse gender identities, using individuals' preferred pronouns. This simple act of respect can enhance credibility and rapport with your audience. One helpful practice is conducting language audits, where you review your content to identify and replace non-inclusive terms. This exercise helps ensure your language is respectful and considerate of all identities. Additionally, reflecting on your language choices encourages mindfulness, helping you become more aware of the impact your words can have.

Examples of effective inclusive language use abound, from corporate diversity initiatives to public addresses by forward-thinking leaders. Companies that prioritize inclusivity often see improved employee satisfaction and engagement. They create policies that promote diverse voices, ensuring everyone feels valued. Public figures who use inclusive language set a powerful example, demonstrating how language can unite rather than divide. Their speeches resonate with a broader audience, illustrating the power of words in shaping a more inclusive society. By learning from these examples, you can refine your communication approach, making it more inclusive and impactful.

Reflection Exercise: Evaluating Your Language Use

Take a moment to reflect on your recent communications. Consider the following questions:

- Are there any gender-specific terms you frequently use that could be replaced with neutral alternatives?
- How often do you check in with your audience to ensure your language aligns with their preferences?
- What steps can you take to increase your awareness of gender-inclusive language and its importance?

Encouraging feedback from diverse audiences can also enhance your understanding. Actively seek input from those with different perspectives to understand how your language choices affect them. This feedback loop helps you grow as a communicator and strengthens your connection with your audience, fostering a more inclusive dialogue.

Balancing Assertiveness and Approachability

Navigating the fine line between assertiveness and approachability can be particularly tricky. This discrepancy can create challenges for both genders, as the expectations and reactions differ significantly, impacting how the audience connects with the speaker. The key lies in finding a balance where authority does not overshadow approachability, allowing for a powerful and engaging message.

To achieve this balance, it's helpful to employ techniques that soften assertive statements while maintaining their impact. One method is to blend directness with empathy, ensuring your message is clear and relatable. Inclusive language and inviting audience interaction can soften your delivery without compromising authority. Building rapport through personal anecdotes can also humanize your message, transforming a rigid monologue into a relatable dialogue. Sharing stories highlighting vulnerability or personal growth makes you approachable, fostering a connection that encourages trust and engagement. These strategies help maintain authority while opening pathways for meaningful audience interaction.

Consider the speeches of Michelle Obama, where assertiveness and approachability coexist in harmony. Her ability to communicate with strength and sincerity allows her to engage audiences profoundly. She shares personal stories illustrating her points, making her messages relatable and resonant. Similarly, Richard Branson's leadership talks exemplify this balance. His direct communication style is tempered with humor and personal insights, creating an engaging atmosphere where authority and approachability thrive together. These examples demonstrate that the most effective communicators are those who can assert their ideas while remaining open and relatable.

Continuous practice and feedback are invaluable in mastering this balance. Participating in communication workshops offers opportunities to refine your approach and experiment with different techniques in a supportive environment. Engaging in peer review sessions provides constructive criticism, allowing you to understand how others perceive your delivery. This feedback loop is essential for growth, offering insights that help you adjust your style to better connect with your audience. The goal is not to change who you are but to enhance how you communicate, ensuring your message is both authoritative and approachable. Through practice and reflection, you can develop a speaking style that resonates deeply, paving the way for impactful and engaging communication.

Balancing assertiveness with approachability is a dynamic process that requires self-awareness and adaptability. It's about cultivating a presence that commands respect while inviting dialogue. As we explore further, remember that mastering this balance is not about conforming to expectations but about finding your unique voice in the spectrum of communication.

Chapter 9

Digital vs. In-Person Speaking Techniques

I magine you're about to deliver a presentation, but instead of standing in a bustling conference room, you find yourself facing a tiny lens, the virtual gatekeeper to your audience. Welcome to your digital stage, a realm where public speaking dynamics shift significantly. Unlike the traditional settings where physical presence commands attention, virtual presentations require a different approach. The absence of physical presence and spatial dynamics means you must rely more heavily on visual aids to convey your message effectively. Without the benefit of direct eye contact or body language to engage your audience, the digital stage demands a nuanced understanding of technology and its capabilities to keep your viewers captivated.

The importance of a robust technical setup cannot be overstated. A high-quality webcam and microphone are not just accessories—they're essential tools that can make or break your presentation. Clear visuals and crisp audio are the foundations of a successful virtual presentation, allowing your audience to focus on your content without distractions. A reliable internet connection is equally critical; nothing disrupts engagement more than a frozen screen or choppy audio. Last but not least, lighting is often overlooked. Are you well lit? If not, explore purchasing a clip-on ring light, LED cube, or panel light for your laptop. Preparing for technical challenges in advance ensures you can handle any hiccups smoothly, keeping your presentation on track and your audience engaged. Conducting a sound check before you begin can help identify potential issues with audio clarity, while testing your internet speed can preempt connectivity problems. These steps, though simple, are vital in setting the stage for a seamless presentation.

Technical Setup Checklist

- Test your camera - Do you have a quality webcam?
- Test your audio - Do you have a quality microphone?
- Test your internet connection - Is your internet connection stable?
- Test your lighting - Are you well-lit?

Engagement is the backbone of any successful presentation, and this holds even truer in the digital realm. The challenge lies in maintaining your audience's attention when they are just a click away from distraction. Interactive elements become your best allies here. Utilize chat functions to encourage questions and foster a sense of community among your audience members. Implementing interactive polls or quizzes can transform passive listening into active participation, making your audience feel like they're part of the conversation. This interaction boosts engagement and provides valuable feedback, allowing you to adjust your delivery in real time. Remember, the more involved your audience feels, the more invested they become in your message.

Consider the success of webinars led by industry leaders, where they have mastered the art of engaging audiences online, blending storytelling with technology to create immersive experiences. These live presentations, conducted over the Internet, often incorporate visuals that complement the speaker's narrative, enhancing understanding and retention. They also frequently use real-time polling to gauge audience opinions, tailoring content to meet their interests. These examples demonstrate that virtual presentations can be as impactful as in-person counterparts with the right tools and strategies.

Interactive Element: Crafting Your Virtual Engagement Strategy

1. Identify Your Tools: List the interactive tools you plan to use, such as chat functions or polls.
2. Plan Your Engagement: Describe how you will incorporate these tools into your presentation to enhance interaction.
3. Set Clear Goals: Define what you want to achieve with audience engagement, such as increased participation or feedback.
4. Practice: Conduct a practice session to familiarize yourself with the tools and refine your delivery.
5. Gather Feedback: After the presentation, solicit feedback to assess the effectiveness of your engagement strategy.

Engaging Virtual Audiences: Techniques for Online Interaction

Navigating the realm of virtual presentations can be a bit like juggling. You're trying to maintain the delicate balance of keeping your audience engaged while facing unique challenges. Unlike face-to-face interactions, the digital world strips away immediate feedback —the nods, smiles, or even the furrowed brows that signal engagement or confusion. This lack of immediate response can leave you feeling like you're broadcasting into a void. Add to that the myriad distractions available to your audience at the click of a button, and engaging them becomes a formidable task. It's easy for someone to open a new tab, check emails, or even get lost in a social media scroll. This digital environment demands strategies that not only capture attention but also sustain it over time.

To truly connect with your virtual audience, you need to employ techniques that encourage participation and maintain interest. One effective method is incorporating breakout rooms for small group discussions. These virtual spaces create opportunities for more intimate interactions, allowing participants to engage with the content and each other. It's like inviting them to step out of the crowded auditorium into a cozy huddle where ideas can flow more freely. Participants return to the main session feeling more invested, having shared their thoughts and listened to others. Another powerful tool is interactive presentation software like Mentimeter. This platform allows you to create polls, quizzes, and word clouds in real-time, turning your audience from passive listeners into active contributors. By asking questions or gauging opinions, you create a dynamic dialogue, keeping engagement levels high and making your presentation feel more like a conversation.

Visual content plays a pivotal role in virtual presentations, perhaps even more so than in-person ones. Dynamic slides with minimal text can communicate key points effectively without overwhelming your audience. Think of your slides as the backdrop to your narrative, enhancing rather than overshadowing your message. Infographics and videos can also be incredibly effective, providing visual stimulation that aids comprehension and retention. They can transform complex data into digestible insights or breathe life into abstract concepts. By carefully curating your visual content, you ensure that it complements your spoken words, creating a cohesive and engaging presentation.

Take inspiration from interactive virtual events that have successfully harnessed these techniques. Virtual Q&A panels invite audience members to pose questions, fostering a sense of community and dialogue. These sessions often feature experts who engage directly with participants, answering queries and exploring topics in depth. Live demonstrations and tutorials take it a step further, offering hands-on experiences that captivate and educate. By involving the audience in real-time activities, these events create an immersive environment that holds attention and encourages active participation. Such examples highlight the potential of virtual presentations to not only replicate the effectiveness of in-person events but also offer unique opportunities for interaction and engagement.

Adapting Body Language for the Camera

In the realm of virtual presentations, body language takes on a new dimension. Unlike in-person settings, where your full stature and movements naturally command attention, the digital stage confines you to a smaller frame. This limitation requires a keen awareness of how you present yourself on camera. Framing and camera positioning become crucial. Your camera should be at eye level, capturing your face, neck, and shoulders. This setup not only ensures your gestures remain visible but also mimics direct eye contact, creating a stronger connection with your audience. Within this limited frame, your gestures need to be more deliberate. Exaggerate them slightly to ensure they are visible and impactful, but remain within the bounds of the screen to avoid appearing disjointed or awkward.

The camera can be your ally if you know how to engage with it. Eye contact, though virtual, is vital. Looking directly into the camera lens rather than at your screen can simulate the feeling of direct engagement, making your audience feel seen and acknowledged. It's like having a conversation with a friend, maintaining a connection that transcends the digital barrier. Keep your gestures within view, using your hands to emphasize key points and add dynamism to your presentation. This not only enhances your message but also keeps your audience visually engaged, preventing their attention from wandering.

Facial expressions also play a central role in virtual communication. With the absence of physical presence, your face becomes a focal point. Smiling, for instance, can convey warmth and approachability, breaking down barriers and inviting your audience into your conversation. Enthusiasm can be projected through animated expressions, adding life and energy to your words. These cues become more prominent on camera, where every raise of an eyebrow or nod carries weight. It's the subtleties in your facial expressions that communicate emotions and reinforce your message.

Consider the effectiveness of on-camera body language from newscasters and online educators. News anchors, for instance, master the use of facial expressions to convey the gravity or levity of the stories they deliver. Their eye contact and subtle nods build trust with viewers, establishing a rapport that feels personal despite the medium. Similarly, popular YouTubers engage their audiences with a dynamic presence. They use lively gestures and expressive faces to maintain attention, creating a vibrant and engaging screen presence. Their ability to connect with viewers through a lens is a testament to the power of adapted body language in virtual settings. This approach can transform your virtual presentation from a static monologue into an engaging dialogue.

Bridging the Gap: Transitioning Between Digital and In-Person

In today's world, the ability to transition seamlessly between digital and in-person presentations is a skill that demands agility and awareness. Each format presents its own unique challenges and dynamics. In-person settings are vibrant, filled with real-time feedback and the palpable energy of the audience. You can gauge reactions instantly through body language and adjust your delivery accordingly.

However, digital presentations strip away this immediacy, often leaving you without the luxury of direct audience cues. This shift requires a quick adaptation of skills, as the techniques that captivate a room may not translate as effectively through a screen. In digital spaces, the absence of physical presence means relying more heavily on vocal modulation and visual aids to maintain engagement. The contrast in audience dynamics can be stark, and adjusting your presentation style to suit each environment becomes crucial.

To navigate these transitions effectively, developing a dual-format presentation plan is beneficial. This approach involves creating content that can be easily adapted for both formats, ensuring consistency in your message and effectiveness in delivery. Practicing hybrid presentation skills is key. For instance, honing your ability to project energy and enthusiasm, whether in a packed conference hall or in front of a webcam, can bridge the gap between formats. Adapting content to fit each setting involves more than just tweaking slides; it means considering how your audience will receive and interact with the material. For in-person settings, you might incorporate more audience interaction and physical demonstrations. In contrast, virtual presentations may require clearer visuals and more structured pacing to accommodate the potential for distractions.

Flexibility and adaptability are the cornerstones of successful transitions between these formats. A versatile speaker remains open to the nuances of each medium, ready to pivot between them with ease. Flexibility exercises can help cultivate this adaptability. For instance, practicing your speech with varying levels of formality or adjusting your pacing based on different audience sizes can prepare you for diverse environments. This adaptability ensures that your message remains impactful regardless of the medium. By developing these skills, you position yourself as a speaker who can thrive in any setting, meeting the demands of both digital and in-person audiences.

Consider speakers who excel in both formats, like those from hybrid conferences where presentations are designed for both live and remote participants. These speakers often blend traditional storytelling with innovative technology, creating experiences that resonate across platforms. Educators who teach both online and face-to-face also demonstrate this skill, adeptly shifting between engaging a classroom and captivating an online audience. Their success lies in their ability to understand the strengths and limitations of each format and leverage them to enhance their delivery. Whether you're delivering a keynote at a bustling conference or hosting a webinar from your living room, these strategies equip you to bridge the gap and connect with your audience effectively.

Utilizing Technology: Tools for Effective Presentation Delivery

In today's presentation landscape, technology isn't just an add-on; it's a game-changer. Whether speaking to a room full of people or addressing an online audience, the right tools can elevate your delivery and engagement levels. Presentation software like PowerPoint and Keynote have become staples in both digital and in-person settings. These platforms offer a range of features that allow you to create visually engaging slides, incorporate animations, and integrate multimedia elements. They help structure your message in a way that is easy for the audience to follow. Meanwhile, audience engagement platforms like Slido enhance interaction by allowing real-time polls and Q&A sessions. These tools transform passive listening into active participation, fostering a two-way communication channel with your audience.

Choosing the right technology for your presentation involves more than just picking the latest gadgets. It's about understanding what will serve you and your audience best. Consider the compatibility of these tools with the devices your audience will likely use. For instance, some platforms work seamlessly across different operating systems, while others might pose challenges. Ease of use is another factor. A tool that offers advanced features but is complicated to navigate can detract from your presentation rather than enhance it. Additionally, accessibility should be a priority. Tools that offer features like screen readers or closed captioning can make your presentation more inclusive, ensuring that everyone can engage fully with your content.

Technology can significantly boost engagement by making your presentation more interactive. For example, augmented reality (AR) offers your audience a deeper layer of interaction. By overlaying digital elements onto the real world, it can create an immersive experience that captivates and educates. Virtual reality (VR) demonstrations, on the other hand, have taken this a step further by allowing audiences to explore topics in a three-dimensional space, offering a level of immersion that more traditional presentations can't match. These examples illustrate the potential of technology to transform how we communicate, making our messages more compelling and our interactions more meaningful.

Managing Technical Difficulties with Poise

Technical issues can arise in any presentation, whether digital or in-person, and they often seem to strike at the most inopportune moments. Connectivity issues are a common culprit, particularly in virtual settings. You might find yourself mid-sentence when your internet connection decides to take a break, leaving you frozen on screen while your audience waits in silence. Equipment malfunctions, such as a microphone suddenly refusing to work or a projector failing to display your slides, can also throw a wrench in your carefully laid plans. These challenges can disrupt the flow of your presentation and test your composure. Recognizing these potential pitfalls is the first step in preparing to handle them with confidence.

To minimize the risk of technical disruptions, thorough preparation is key. Conducting pre-event technical checks can help identify and address potential issues before they become problems. This includes testing your equipment, checking your internet speed, and ensuring all necessary software is updated and functioning properly. Having a backup plan is also wise. Consider preparing an extra set of slides on a USB drive or having a second device ready to connect online if needed. Familiarize yourself with the venue or platform you'll be using so you're not caught off guard by unfamiliar technology. These proactive measures may seem tedious, but they are invaluable in maintaining the integrity of your presentation.

Even with the best preparation, technical issues can still arise, and how you handle them can leave a lasting impression on your audience. Maintaining composure is crucial. A calm demeanor not only reassures your audience but also helps you think clearly and solve the problem efficiently. Communicate openly with your audience about the issue, keeping them informed while you work to resolve it. Transparency builds trust and shows professionalism. Keep your tone steady and your body language relaxed—this signals to your audience that you are in control, even if things aren't going as planned.

Consider the example of a conference speaker who faced an unexpected glitch when the presentation slides refused to load. Instead of panicking, the speaker engaged the audience with an impromptu story related to the topic, buying time while the technical team worked on the issue. Quick-thinking and a calm approach keeps the audience engaged and showcases adaptability. Similarly, virtual presenters who encounter connectivity issues can use humor or share insights verbally to maintain engagement while reconnecting. By addressing technical difficulties with poise and creativity, you turn potential setbacks into opportunities for connection and demonstrate your ability to handle pressure.

Chapter 10

Leveraging Public Speaking for Career Advancement

Imagine entering a room where every eye is on you, not with skepticism but anticipation. You've been invited to speak because your words carry weight, and your ideas inspire action. This isn't just a dream scenario for leaders; it's a powerful reality. Public speaking is more than just a tool—it's a pillar of effective leadership, enabling you to articulate visions, inspire teams, and drive change. Whether you're addressing a small team or a large audience, the ability to communicate clearly and persuasively is what sets successful leaders apart.

In the realm of leadership, the spoken word is a powerful motivator. Leaders who can inspire through motivational and inspirational speaking have a distinct advantage. They create environments where teams are not just informed but also empowered to act. When you communicate clearly, you eliminate ambiguity, allowing team members to navigate their tasks purposefully. Clarity is necessary for building trust and fostering a culture of open communication. Your ability to articulate a clear vision is what aligns your team, ensuring everyone is moving toward a common goal. Public speaking is your medium for conveying that vision, transforming abstract ideas into tangible objectives that your team can rally around.

Consider influential leaders who have used speeches to drive significant change. These leaders understand that words can ignite movements and inspire action. Martin Luther King Jr.'s "I Have a Dream" speech didn't just articulate a vision for equality—it mobilized a nation to strive for change. Similarly, Steve Jobs' product launches were more than presentations; they were calls to innovation that redefined industries. These leaders didn't just speak; they connected with their audiences on a deeper level, using their words as tools for transformation. Through public addresses, they inspired others to embrace their vision and work toward a shared future.

Crafting a persuasive leadership style involves more than choosing the right words. It's about aligning your message with organizational goals and using storytelling to illustrate principles. Stories are powerful because they resonate with our innate desire for connection. When you incorporate storytelling into your speeches, you make your message relatable and memorable. This technique doesn't just engage your audience; it also reinforces your leadership principles, making your vision accessible and compelling. Crafting speeches that align with organizational goals ensures that your message is not only heard but also acted upon.

Developing a leadership communication style that reflects your brand is crucial for establishing your presence. Start by identifying the personal leadership qualities you want to emphasize. Are you known for your empathy, decisiveness, or innovation? Let these traits guide how you communicate. Your style should reflect who you are as a leader, embracing authenticity while adapting to the needs of your audience. Cultivating this style requires introspection and practice, but the result is a unique voice that resonates with those you lead. Embrace the opportunity to refine your approach, and let your communication reflect the leader you aspire to be.

Reflection Exercise: Identify Your Leadership Qualities

Take a moment to reflect on what makes you a unique leader. Consider the qualities that define your leadership style. Are you a visionary who inspires through innovation, or do you lead with empathy and understanding? Write down three qualities that you believe are your strengths. Then, consider how these qualities can be woven into your communication style. How can you use them to connect with your audience and convey your vision effectively? This exercise will help you align your speaking style with your leadership brand, ensuring that the words you speak reinforce the leader you are.

Networking Through Speaking Engagements

Imagine standing in front of an audience, sharing your insights and expertise. The spotlight is on you; every word you speak is an opportunity to connect with others who share your interests and ambitions. Speaking engagements offer a unique platform for networking, allowing you to build credibility and engage with industry leaders. When you share your knowledge, you position yourself as an expert in your field, inviting others to view you as a valuable resource. Credibility is crucial in today's competitive environment, where trust and reputation can open doors to new opportunities. Engaging with industry leaders at conferences broadens your network and exposes you to various perspectives and ideas, enriching your own understanding and sparking innovation.

Choosing the right speaking opportunities is key to maximizing your networking potential. Not all events are created equal, so it's important to select forums that align with your career goals and networking needs. Start by identifying relevant industry events and panels that attract the audience you want to connect with. Consider the topics you are passionate about and how they align with the event's theme. This alignment ensures that your message resonates with the audi-

ence and that you engage with like-minded professionals who share similar interests. Researching the attendee list can also provide valuable insights into potential contacts, allowing you to tailor your message to their interests and needs.

Once you've secured a speaking engagement, it's time to maximize your networking efforts. Initiating and nurturing professional relationships through speaking requires a thoughtful approach. Begin by clearly articulating your message and demonstrating your expertise. This not only captures the audience's attention but also establishes your credibility. As you interact with attendees, be genuine and approachable, fostering an environment where connections can flourish. One effective strategy is to follow up with contacts you've made, expressing gratitude for their time and interest. Following up can be as simple as sending a personalized email or connecting on LinkedIn to continue the conversation. You lay the groundwork for future collaborations and opportunities by nurturing these relationships.

The importance of visibility in career growth cannot be overstated. Public speaking enhances your professional visibility, increasing your influence and positioning you as a known expert in your field. As you continue to engage with audiences through speaking engagements, your reputation grows, attracting new opportunities and expanding your network. Visibility not only boosts your career prospects but also empowers you to contribute to your industry meaningfully. Becoming a known expert means that when people think of your field, they think of you as a go-to resource, someone whose insights and opinions are valued and respected. Recognition can often lead to invitations to speak at other events, write for industry publications, or even collaborate on projects that align with your interests and expertise.

Public speaking is a powerful networking and professional growth tool in this dynamic landscape. Choosing the right opportunities and engaging with your audience can build a network that supports and enhances your career. You can share your voice, connect with others, and leave a lasting impact.

Crafting an Elevator Pitch that Stands Out

Imagine for a moment stepping into an elevator and finding yourself face-to-face with the CEO of a company that you've always dreamed about working with. You have just a few floors' worth of time to make a lasting impression. The elevator pitch shines in this scenario—a concise, compelling introduction that opens doors to career opportunities. It's your chance to showcase who you are, what you do, and where you want to go in a matter of seconds. The key components include a strong opening that grabs attention, a clear statement of what you offer, and a call to action that leaves your listener wanting more. An effective elevator pitch is not just about cramming information into 30 seconds; it's about distilling your essence into a memorable soundbite.

Creating a memorable pitch begins with careful reflection on your unique skills and value. Start by identifying your core strengths and achievements. Consider the goals you've accomplished that set you apart in your field. These personal achievements are your selling points—the aspects of your career that make you a standout candidate. Now, think about your professional goals. How do your skills align with where you want to be? This alignment is crucial as it shows forward-thinking and ambition. Weave these elements into a narrative that speaks to your expertise and aspirations. Your pitch should paint a picture of your potential, leaving your listener intrigued and eager to learn more.

Delivery is where your pitch comes to life. Voice modulation, body language, and timing play pivotal roles in conveying confidence and engagement. Practice your pitch aloud, paying attention to the nuances of your voice. Is your tone inviting? Does your pitch have the right rhythm? Avoid a monotone delivery by varying your pitch to emphasize key points. Body language is equally important. Be sure to stand tall, make eye contact, and use gestures that reinforce your words. These non-verbal cues add an extra layer of impact to your message. Timing is crucial—your pitch should feel natural and unrushed, even if time is short. Engaging language captivates listeners, creating a connection that transforms a brief encounter into a meaningful exchange.

Consider the example of a successful entrepreneur who crafted a pitch that led to a pivotal business breakthrough. Standing at a networking event, she introduced herself not as just another tech founder but as someone who "turns complex data into actionable insights that drive profitability." This pitch was succinct yet powerful, highlighting her unique value proposition. Her engaging delivery, coupled with a genuine smile and confident stance, left a lasting impression. As a result, she secured a meeting with a potential investor intrigued by her approach. Simple yet effective pitches open doors to new opportunities, this demonstrates the power of a well-crafted introduction.

Public Speaking for Professional Growth and Recognition

Public speaking is a cornerstone for career advancement. It's not merely about sharing knowledge; it's a stage where you can showcase your expertise and gain recognition. Think of keynote addresses. They are golden opportunities to establish yourself as an authority in your field. When you stand before an audience, articulating your insights and vision, you aren't just speaking; you're shaping your professional narrative. This visibility can lead to promotions, as decision-makers often recognize and reward those who can effectively communicate their ideas. A well-delivered speech can position you as a thought leader, opening doors to new opportunities and collaborations.

Building a speaking portfolio is an essential step in leveraging public speaking for career growth. Start by documenting your speaking engagements. Keep a record of each event, noting the audience size, topics covered, and feedback received. This record serves as tangible proof of your experience and expertise. Creating a professional speaker profile can further enhance your credibility. Include a bio that highlights your achievements and areas of expertise. A well-crafted profile showcases your speaking history and sets you apart from others. Collect testimonials from event organizers and attendees to reinforce your impact and effectiveness. Positive feedback serves as social proof, encouraging future engagements and endorsements.

Public speaking can be a powerful tool for career transitions. If you're looking to move into a new role or industry, speaking engagements allow you to demonstrate your expertise and adaptability. By sharing insights and experiences that resonate with your target audience, you can build connections that facilitate your transition. Use these opportunities to highlight your transferable skills and how they apply to the new field. Such an approach not only showcases your versatility but also positions you as a valuable asset, capable of bringing fresh perspectives and ideas to different sectors. Speaking engagements become a platform for you to redefine your professional identity and expand your horizons.

Seeking speaking opportunities requires a proactive approach. Start by networking with event organizers and industry leaders. Attend conferences and seminars where you can connect with key decision-makers. Express your interest in speaking and propose topics that align with the event's theme. Demonstrate how your insights can add value to the audience. Crafting tailored pitches can increase your chances of being invited to speak. Highlight your expertise and the unique perspectives you bring. Furthermore, leverage social media and professional networks to showcase your speaking engagements.

Sharing clips or highlights from your talks can attract attention and lead to more invitations.

Public speaking is a dynamic tool that can elevate your career and enhance your professional recognition. By building a strong speaking portfolio, leveraging opportunities for career transitions, and actively seeking engagements, you can position yourself as a leader in your field. This process is about more than just speaking; it's about creating a lasting impression that resonates with your audience and influences your career trajectory. As you continue to hone your skills and expand your network, you'll find that public speaking becomes an integral part of your professional identity, enriching both your career and personal growth.

Transforming Public Speaking Skills into Career Assets

In the business world, communication skills are a significant asset, often dictating the trajectory of one's career. The ability to convey ideas clearly and persuasively is not just a nice-to-have; it's a cornerstone of professional competency. Public speaking enhances your negotiation skills by teaching you to present compelling arguments and respond to counter arguments with poise. Imagine being in a high-stakes meeting where every word counts. Your ability to articulate your position confidently can make the difference between closing a deal and missing an opportunity. This skill extends into meeting facilitation, where guiding discussions with clarity and purpose can lead to more productive outcomes. A well-facilitated meeting aligns team members, ensuring everyone understands their roles and tasks.

Integrating speaking skills into daily work is a practice that can elevate your professional presence. Consider your role in team meetings. When you lead with clarity and confidence, you set the tone for the session, encouraging participation and fostering a collaborative environment. Your team looks to you for guidance, and your communication style can either inspire or inhibit their contributions. Similarly, when presenting projects and proposals, your ability to communicate persuasively can influence stakeholders' decisions. A well-delivered presentation can convince even the most skeptical audience of your project's value and potential. You enhance your effectiveness and demonstrate leadership by weaving speaking skills into these everyday scenarios.

Continuous improvement is the key to maintaining and expanding your speaking competencies. The world of communication is ever-evolving, and staying ahead requires dedication to learning. Participating in workshops and training sessions can introduce you to new techniques and perspectives. These opportunities provide a platform for practice and feedback, crucial components for honing your skills. Engaging with your peers and experts allows you to refine your approach, ensuring your communication style remains relevant and impactful. Embrace these learning experiences to challenge yourself and grow, knowing that each step forward enhances your ability to connect and influence.

To illustrate the power of public speaking in career advancement, consider the story of a professional who transitioned to a leadership role through their speaking abilities. Initially working in a technical field, they realized their insights were often overlooked because they struggled to communicate them effectively. Determined to change this, they invested time in developing their speaking skills, attending workshops, and seeking mentorship. They began sharing their ideas more openly with newfound confidence, leading to recognition and opportunities within their organization. As they continued to speak at industry events, their reputation as a thought leader grew, culminating in a promotion to a leadership position where they now guide their team with the same clarity and conviction they once sought.

In this chapter, we've explored how public speaking skills can be a powerful asset in your career toolkit. From enhancing professional competency to integrating these skills into daily work, the impact is profound. Continuous learning ensures you remain at the forefront, ready to seize opportunities that come your way. Consider how these skills can further enrich your professional journey. How could public speaking open doors to new possibilities and inspired challenges in your career?

Chapter 11

Embracing Continuous Improvement and Lifelong Learning

Picture a marathon runner at the starting line, poised to begin a long race. Every stride is deliberate, each step building on the last, moving toward a distant finish. Public speaking and self-improvement are much like that marathon—continuous, challenging, but ultimately rewarding. Becoming a compelling speaker isn't a sprint; it's about setting achievable goals and steadily working towards them. These goals act as milestones, guiding your journey and inspiring you to grow. Imagine the sense of accomplishment you'll feel as you tick off each box, knowing you're not just speaking but communicating with purpose and clarity.

Setting specific, measurable goals is crucial for growth in public speaking. Without clear objectives, you risk wandering aimlessly, unsure of what you want to achieve. This is where the SMART (Specific, Measurable, Attainable, Relevant, and Time-Bound) framework comes into play. Instead of vaguely wishing to "be a better speaker," a SMART goal might be "to reduce filler words to two per ten-minute speech within four months" (SOURCE 1). This clarity transforms abstract desires into actionable plans, helping you focus your efforts and track your progress.

Begin by defining what you wish to accomplish in your public speaking endeavors. Consider writing a personal public speaking mission statement. This statement acts as your guiding star, aligning your speaking activities with your broader life goals. Next, create a list of skills you want to develop—perhaps improving your posture or enhancing audience engagement. Each skill represents a step toward your overarching mission, bringing you closer to your ideal speaker persona.

Tracking your progress is essential to understand where you stand and how far you've come. Consider keeping a journal dedicated to your speaking journey. Document each speaking experience, noting what went well and areas for improvement. This practice not only highlights your achievements but also helps identify patterns that might be holding you back. Over time, this journal becomes invaluable, offering insights into your growth and areas that need attention.

Flexibility is key in goal setting. As you evolve, so too should your goals. Life is dynamic, and unexpected challenges or opportunities may arise. Be ready to revisit and adjust your objectives as needed. Perhaps you initially aimed to enhance your vocal modulation, but as you progress, you realize that engaging storytelling is a more pressing need. Adapting your goals ensures they remain relevant and challenging, pushing you to continually stretch your capabilities.

Journaling Prompt: Reflective Goal Setting

1. Define Your Mission: Write a brief personal mission statement for your public speaking journey. Consider your motivations and what you hope to achieve.
2. Skill List: Identify three speaking skills you want to improve. Why are these important to you?
3. Reflect on Progress: After each speaking engagement, jot down what went well and what you'd like to work on. Use this reflection to adjust your goals as needed.

By setting clear goals, tracking progress, and staying flexible, you'll soon find yourself speaking, engaging, inspiring, and leading with confidence.

Creating a Personal Development Plan for Speaking

Think of your personal development plan (PDP) as a roadmap, guiding you through the sophisticated landscape of public speaking. This plan is a strategic outline for enhancing your skills and advancing your career. It's not just about setting goals; it's about crafting a structured path that aligns with your aspirations. An effective PDP for speakers includes several components: a clear understanding of your current abilities, a realistic set of goals, a timeline for achievement, and a list of resources for learning. This plan is your personalized guide, helping you navigate the complexities of public speaking with confidence and clarity.

Identifying areas for improvement starts with a thorough self-assessment. Reflect on your speaking experiences. What are your strengths, and where do you feel less confident? Pinpointing these areas can be enlightening. You might realize that while your storytelling captivates, your posture needs work. Seeking input from mentors and peers can also provide valuable insights. A trusted colleague might notice nuances in your delivery that you overlook. Their feedback can highlight blind spots and reinforce strengths, offering a more holistic view of your abilities.

Once you've identified your development areas, it's time to create an actionable PDP. Setting realistic timelines and milestones is crucial. Break your goals into smaller, manageable tasks. For instance, if you want to enhance your vocal variety, start with exercises focusing on pitch and tone, aiming for noticeable improvement over three months. Schedule regular review sessions to assess your progress. These reviews are opportunities to reflect, adjust, and celebrate achievements. They keep you accountable and motivated, ensuring you're continually moving forward.

Learning resources are integral to your development plan. Books, courses, and workshops provide knowledge and skills that can transform your speaking abilities. Curate a list of recommended resources, focusing on those that align with your goals. A book on storytelling or a course on body language could be beneficial. Workshops offer hands-on experience and the chance to practice in a supportive environment. These resources are about acquiring new skills and refining and enhancing what you already know, pushing you toward excellence.

Incorporating these elements into your PDP creates a dynamic framework that evolves with you. It's not a static document but a living guide that adapts as you grow and change. Embrace the flexibility to adjust your plan as needed. Life is unpredictable, and opportunities may lead you in unexpected directions. Your PDP should reflect this fluidity, evolving alongside your career and personal growth.

Utilizing Feedback for Continuous Improvement

Imagine you're standing on stage, delivering a speech that feels just right. The audience is engaged, nodding along, but how do you know if your delivery truly hit the mark? This is where the power of feedback comes into play. Constructive feedback serves as a mirror, reflecting your strengths and areas needing improvement. It's a vital tool for growth, offering insights that you might overlook. Positive feedback highlights what works well, reinforcing effective techniques. However, negative feedback, often perceived as criticism, is equally crucial. It shines a light on blind spots, guiding you toward refinement. Differentiating the two allows you to build on your successes while addressing weaknesses, creating a balanced approach to improvement.

Seeking meaningful feedback requires a proactive approach. Start by setting up feedback sessions with trusted colleagues who understand your speaking goals and can offer honest, actionable insights. These sessions should be a safe space for open dialogue, where constructive criticism is welcomed. Additionally, using feedback forms after presentations can provide diverse perspectives. Tailor these forms to capture specific areas you are working on, such as delivery style or engagement techniques. Encourage feedback from various sources, including peers, mentors, and even audience members, to gather a comprehensive view of your performance. This diverse input ensures you receive well-rounded insights crucial for continuous development.

Once you've gathered feedback, the next step is interpreting and applying it effectively. Analyze the comments, looking for recurring themes or patterns. If several people mention the same issue, such as a tendency to rush through key points, this indicates an area to prioritize for change. Use this information to refine your approach, experimenting with different techniques to see what resonates best.

Constructive feedback isn't just about pointing out flaws; it's a roadmap for improvement. By implementing these suggestions, you enhance your skills and demonstrate a commitment to excellence. Feedback catalyzes transformation, propelling you toward your public speaking goals.

Adopting a feedback-positive mindset is essential. View feedback as a tool for empowerment rather than criticism. Such a perspective shift allows you to embrace feedback with resilience and openness. Recognize that everyone has areas to improve, and feedback is a mechanism to facilitate growth. It's not personal; it's a stepping stone to becoming a more effective communicator. Developing this mindset takes practice, but it's a worthwhile endeavor. Embracing feedback with gratitude and curiosity transforms it from a source of anxiety into a powerful ally in your journey toward public speaking mastery. This openness to feedback enhances your skills and fosters a culture of continuous learning and adaptation, essential in any professional setting.

Staying Updated with Latest Public Speaking Trends

Envision yourself confidently taking the stage, armed not only with a compelling message but also with the latest tools and techniques at your disposal. Keeping abreast of the newest trends in public speaking can profoundly boost your effectiveness. In an environment that constantly evolves, propelled by technological innovations, how we communicate and connect is continually being reshaped. Being aware of these trends means you're not just keeping pace with the world but setting the stage to lead it. Technological advancements, in particular, have revolutionized public speaking. From interactive presentations that captivate audiences to virtual reality experiences that immerse them in your message, these innovations offer new ways to engage and inspire. Virtual presentations have become a staple, reshaping how we reach audiences globally, while

AI-driven tools can tailor presentations to better meet audience needs.

Identifying emerging trends requires a proactive approach. Social media is an invaluable resource for spotting these shifts. By following industry leaders, you gain insights into what's shaping the future of public speaking. These thought leaders often share their experiences and predictions, offering a glimpse into the cutting-edge techniques they use. Public speaking journals and newsletters are another treasure trove of information. Subscribing to these publications informs you about the latest research and best practices. They provide detailed analyses and case studies, helping you understand how trends are applied in real-world scenarios. Conferences, whether in-person or virtually, offer a platform to learn from experts and peers alike. These gatherings highlight innovative approaches and provide a collaborative space to exchange ideas and strategies.

Staying current isn't merely about keeping up; it's about embracing opportunities to enhance your effectiveness and connect more deeply with your audience.

Engaging with Public Speaking Communities for Growth

Imagine stepping into a room full of people who share your passion for public speaking. These gatherings, whether in person or online, offer a space where individuals come together, united by their desire to improve and inspire. Engaging with public speaking communities provides more than just a platform for practice; it offers a network of support and inspiration. In these groups, you'll find peers who understand your challenges and mentors who guide you, offering insights born from experience. Networking opportunities abound, allowing you to connect with like-minded individuals who can become collaborators, mentors, or even friends. Peer learning is a cornerstone of these communities, as each member brings unique perspectives and experiences that enrich the collective knowledge. By sharing successes and setbacks, you gain new strategies and insights, fostering a culture of mutual growth and encouragement.

Finding and joining these communities is easier than you might think. Organizations like Toastmasters International have chapters worldwide, providing structured environments to hone your speaking skills. These groups offer regular meetings where members practice prepared and impromptu speeches, receiving  constructive feedback in a supportive setting. Online forums and discussion groups are also invaluable resources. Platforms such as LinkedIn or specialized public speaking forums connect you with experts and enthusiasts around the globe. Participating in these online spaces allows you to engage in discussions, share resources, and even find virtual speaking opportunities. The key is to be proactive—seek out groups that line up with your interests and goals, and don't hesitate to reach out and introduce yourself. Becoming an active member of these communities can open doors to opportunities you hadn't considered, broadening your horizons and deepening your understanding of public speaking.

Once you're part of a community, the real growth begins. Contributing your experiences and insights not only helps others but reinforces your own learning. Presenting at local meetups or workshops provides valuable practice and feedback, allowing you to refine your skills in a real-world setting. Collaboration with community members on projects or events can lead to innovative ideas and new opportunities. These collaborative efforts often result in creative solutions and increased confidence as you learn to navigate diverse perspectives and approaches. Sharing your journey encourages others to do the same, creating a cycle of continuous improvement and support. The relationships you build in these communities can become a vital network, offering guidance and encouragement as you progress in your public speaking endeavors.

Mentorship and collaboration are integral to personal growth within these communities. Experienced speakers can offer guidance and feedback, helping you navigate challenges and develop your unique voice. Seeking mentorship provides personalized learning and growth opportunities tailored to your specific needs and goals. A mentor can offer insights gained from years of experience, helping you avoid common pitfalls and accelerate your development. Collaboration among peers fosters a sense of camaraderie and shared purpose. Working together on projects or presentations lets you learn from each other's strengths and experiences, enhancing your skills and broadening your perspective. Whether you're collaborating with peers or receiving guidance from a mentor, these relationships are invaluable resources that support your journey toward becoming a more confident and effective speaker.

Celebrating Milestones on Your Speaking Journey

Acknowledging public speaking milestones can be just as exhilarating as reaching the summit after a long climb. Recognizing achievements isn't just about patting yourself on the back—it's about reinforcing your progress. When you pause to celebrate, you affirm your efforts and fuel your motivation to tackle the next challenge. Recognition is vital, it offers psychological benefits that boost confidence and reinforce your commitment to growth—every milestone, whether big or small, is a testament to your dedication and hard work. As you celebrate, you're reminded of where you started and how far you've come, reinforcing the belief in your ability to keep moving forward.

Celebrating these milestones can take many forms, each tailored to what resonates with you. Consider hosting a small gathering with friends, colleagues, or fellow speakers to share your recent successes. Such gatherings aren't about boasting but sharing your journey with those who support and inspire you. It creates a sense of community and belonging, strengthening the bonds that sustain you through challenges. Alternatively, mark your achievements with a personal reward, such as a special dinner or a day dedicated to your favorite hobby. These celebrations function as reminders of your progress and accomplishments, providing a moment to reflect and recharge before setting your sights on new goals.

After celebrating, it's time to look ahead. Use these milestones as springboards to set new challenges. Take a moment to evaluate your progress, considering what worked well and what could be improved. Reflection is an opportunity to plan your next steps strategically. Perhaps you've mastered storytelling, and now it's time to focus on enhancing your vocal variety. By analyzing your achievements, you can set tailored goals that build on your strengths and address areas for growth. These new challenges keep you engaged and motivated, ensuring that your journey in public speaking remains dynamic and fulfilling.

Exercise

Write a reflection piece on your key accomplishments, considering the obstacles you overcame and the skills you developed. This exercise isn't just about looking back—it's about gaining insights that inform your future endeavors. Reflecting on your journey helps you identify patterns and strategies that lead to success, reinforcing your confidence and resilience. It also allows you to acknowledge the support and guidance you've received, fostering gratitude and strengthening relationships.

Celebrating milestones is more than a momentary pause; it's a vital practice that nourishes your growth and inspires continued progress. As you embrace each achievement, remember that these milestones are stepping stones to becoming a more confident and effective speaker.

Keeping the Game Alive

Now that you have everything you need to become a confident, engaging speaker, it's time to pay it forward and help others find their voice too.

By leaving an honest review of this book on Amazon, you'll show other aspiring speakers where they can find the guidance they need to overcome their fears and master the art of public speaking.

Thank you for your support. Public speaking thrives when we pass on our knowledge, and by leaving a review, together we are doing just that.

Click here to leave your review on Amazon.

Conclusion

As we reach the end of this journey, it's time to look back and see just how much you've learned. We've explored the vast landscape of public speaking, equipping you with a toolkit filled with practical strategies and insights. From managing stage fright to crafting captivating speeches, you've learned how to confidently stand in front of any audience and deliver your message with impact.

Remember those initial fears? The heart pounding, the palms sweating, the uncertainty of how your words would land? Those nerves are no longer a barrier. You've learned how to turn them into strengths. Techniques like diaphragmatic breathing and visualization have become your allies, helping you to calm your mind and engage your audience with poise and presence.

Crafting engaging speeches will now be second nature to you. You've discovered the art of storytelling, the power of structuring your speech with the Hero's Journey or the Three-Act Structure. These aren't just tools; they're keys to unlocking the hearts and minds of your listeners. Your words can now resonate, leaving an indelible mark long after the speech has ended.

But it doesn't stop there. Mastering vocal dynamics has opened new doors. Whether varying your pitch to emphasize a point or using pauses effectively to let your message sink in, your voice is a powerful instrument. You've learned to use it wisely, engaging your audience and holding their attention with every syllable.

Tailoring your message for diverse audiences is another skill you will embrace. You've learned to navigate gender dynamics, adapt your style for digital versus in-person settings, and create inclusive environments that invite participation and dialogue. Your speeches will now connect with people on a deeper level, fostering understanding and rapport.

This book has also highlighted the role of public speaking in career growth. You've seen how effective communication can open doors to new opportunities, enhance your leadership presence, and position you as an authority in your field. By leveraging these skills, you're not just speaking but leading, inspiring, and influencing others.

Yet, the journey doesn't end here. Public speaking is a lifelong endeavor. It's about continuous improvement, constantly pushing the boundaries of what you can achieve. Remember to reflect on your progress, celebrate milestones, and set new goals. Each step forward is a testament to your commitment to growth and excellence.

Above all, stay true to yourself. Authenticity is your greatest asset. By embracing your authentic voice and personal branding, you forge genuine connections with your audience. Imperfections make you relatable, and vulnerability strengthens trust. Your unique perspective is a gift—share it boldly and confidently.

As you come to the end of this book, take a moment to celebrate the progress you've made. Each chapter is a building block, shaping you into the speaker you are today and will continue to become in the future. You've practiced or will practice, reflect, and grow, and that's worth acknowledging. Let this be a reminder of your dedication and resilience.

Now, it's time for action. Apply the practical strategies you've learned one by one. Seek new speaking opportunities at work, in your community, or on a larger stage. Each experience will hone your skills and bring you closer to your speaking goals. Envision the future—a future where you stand as a skilled speaker, influencing, leading, and inspiring those around you.

Thank you for trusting me to guide you on this journey. Your dedication to enhancing your public speaking abilities is commendable. You've shown a commitment to growth, and that will serve you well in all your endeavors.

As you continue this journey, let these words from Ralph Waldo Emerson guide you: "Speech is power: speech is to persuade, to convert, to compel." May your words carry the power to change minds, touch hearts, and inspire action. Your voice matters, and the world is waiting to hear it.

References

Abbajay, M. (2020). *Best practices for virtual presentations: 15 expert tips.* Forbes. https://www.forbes.com/sites/maryabbajay/2020/04/20/best-practices-for-virtual-presentations-15-expert-tips-that-work-for-everyone/

Bartlett, E. (2022). *8 classic storytelling techniques for engaging presentations.* Sparkol. https://blog.sparkol.com/8-classic-storytelling-techniques-for-engaging-presentations

Canadian Western Bank. (2023). *7 tips for delivering inclusive presentations.* Canadian Western Bank. https://www.cwbank.com/en/blog/7-tips-for-delivering-inclusive-presentations

Chapman, C. (n.d.). *A complete overview of the best data visualization tools.* Toptal Designers. https://www.toptal.com/designers/data-visualization/data-visualization-tools

Chen, N. I. (n.d.). *8 steps to eliminating filler words - Speak as a leader.* Speaking Coach. https://www.speaking.coach/simple-strategies-to-eliminate-filler-words-and-improve-any-presentation/

Cohan, P. (2023). *Takeaways from 3 great Steve Jobs stories.* Inc. https://www.inc.com/peter-cohan/takeaways-from-3-great-steve-jobs-stories.html

Cubicle Ninjas. (n.d.). *25 examples of rhetorical strategies in famous speeches.* Cubicle Ninjas. https://cubicleninjas.com/25-examples-of-rhetorical-strategies/

Dalumpines, M. (2024). *The ultimate guide to audience engagement tools.* Canapii. https://canapii.com/blog/the-ultimate-guide-to-audience-engagement-tools/

Decastro, M. (2018). *Oprah Winfrey - Public speaking at its finest: I – Inspire.* Mindful Presenter. https://mindfulpresenter.com/oprah-winfrey-public-speaking/

Dhu, P. (n.d.). *9 tips for quickly building rapport with your audience.* LinkedIn. https://www.linkedin.com/pulse/9-tips-quickly-building-rapport-your-audience-peter-dhu-mba-csp

DiResta, D. (n.d.). *The thrilling impact of authenticity in public speaking.* DiResta Communications Inc. https://www.diresta.com/knockoutpresentationsblog/authenticity-the-key-to-powerful-public-speaking

Duarte. (n.d.). *Good business communication demands a 3-act story structure.* Duarte. https://www.duarte.com/blog/business-communication-demands-3-act-story-structure/

Edgar, D. (2013). *"Yes we can" – Barack Obama's lesson in American rhetoric.* The Guardian. https://www.theguardian.com/books/2013/nov/04/barack-obama-lesson-american-rhetoric

Faster Capital. (2024). *Cognitive reframing in practice: Real-life examples and success stories.* Faster Capital. https://fastercapital.com/content/Cognitive-restructuring-and-reframing--Cognitive-Reframing-in-Practice--Real-Life-Examples-and-Success-Stories.html

Freeman, S. (2018). *Gender differences in communication styles*. Freeman Means Business. https://freemanmeansbusiness.com/blog/2018/9/13/gender-differences-in-communication-styles

Goman, C. K. (2019). *10 powerful body language tips*. AMA American Management Association. https://www.amanet.org/articles/10-powerful-body-language-tips/

Gotter, A. (2023). *8 breathing exercises for anxiety you can try right now*. Healthline. https://www.healthline.com/health/breathing-exercises-for-anxiety

Grant, A. (2017). *How vulnerability can help you connect with an audience*. Knowledge at Wharton. https://knowledge.wharton.upenn.edu/article/how-vulnerability-can-help-you-connect-with-an-audience/

Guarino, J. (n.d.). *Prepping for public speaking with creative visualization*. Institute of Public Speaking. https://www.instituteofpublicspeaking.com/prepping-for-public-speaking-with-creative-visualization/

Harvard FAS. (2022). *How to create an elevator pitch with examples*. https://careerservices.fas.harvard.edu/blog/2022/10/11/how-to-create-an-elevator-pitch-with-examples/

Huckle, B. (2021). *6 body language tips when presenting online*. Second Nature. https://www.secondnature.com.au/blog/body-language-tips-for-virtual-presenters/

Indeed Editorial Team. (2023). *Monroe's motivated sequence: Definition, 5 steps and more*. Indeed. https://www.indeed.com/career-advice/career-development/motivated-sequence

Intentional Outcomes Counselling. (n.d.). *Decoding impostor syndrome: Navigating the maze with cognitive behavioral therapy*. Intentional Outcomes Counselling. https://intentionaloutcomes.com/decoding-impostor-syndrome-navigating-the-maze-with-cognitive-behavioral-therapy/#:~:text=Cognitive%20Restructuring%3A%20CBT%20encourages%20individuals,Impostor%20Syndrome%20-can%20be%20mitigated.

Joseph, J. (n.d.). *Why is personal branding essential for keynote speakers?* Dr. Jerome Joseph. https://jeromejoseph.com/why-is-personal-branding-essential-for-keynote-speakers/#:~:text=To%20start%20creating%20your%20personal,establishing%20and%20growing%20your%20brand.

Kinnie, C. M. (2023). *9 speaking industry trends to watch in 2023*. The Speaker Lab. https://thespeakerlab.com/blog/9-speaking-industry-trends-to-watch-in-2023/

Kristenson, S. (2022). *11 SMART goals examples for your public speaking skills*. Develop Good Habits. https://www.developgoodhabits.com/smart-goals-public-speaking/

Li, D. (2024). *How to create a presentation outline (with examples)*. Plus. https://www.plusdocs.com/blog/how-to-create-a-presentation-outline-with-examples

Manzenza International. (n.d.). *Master the art of networking at speaking engagements*. Manzenza International. https://www.manzenzainternational.com/blog/master-the-art-of-networking-at-speaking-engagements

Millen, J. (n.d.). *10 tips to handle difficult questions during your presentation*. John

Millen. https://www.johnmillen.com/blog/10-tips-to-handle-difficult-questions-during-a-presentation

Mitchell, O. (n.d.). *How to prepare for your Q&A session*. Speaking About Presenting. https://speakingaboutpresenting.com/audience/how-to-prepare-for-a-qa-session/

Randolph, M. (n.d.). *14.2: Public Speaking Online Vs. Face-to-Face*. Libre Texts. https://socialsci.libretexts.org/Courses/Fresno_City_College/COMM_1%3A_Introduction_to_Public_Speaking/14%3A_Mediated_Communication/14.02%3A_Public_Speaking_Online_Vs._Face-to-Face#:~:text=of%20your%20voice.-,Nonverbal%20Communication,gestures%2C%20and%20how%20we%20dress.

Resume Way. (2024). *Create an effective personal development plan in 7 steps*. Resume Way. https://www.resumeway.com/blog/personal-development-plan/

Science Direct. (n.d.). *Stage fright - an overview*. ScienceDirect Topics. https://www.sciencedirect.com/topics/psychology/stage-fright

Slidemodel.com. (2025). *47+ best PowerPoint templates & presentation slides*. Slidemodel.com. https://slidemodel.com/best-powerpoint-templates/

Slido. (n.d.). *Audience interaction made easy*. Slido. https://www.slido.com/

Speak Easy. (n.d.). *Effective vocal exercises for speaking*. Speak Easy. https://www.speakeasyinc.com/vocal-exercises-for-speaking/

Speaker Lab. (2024). *The power of the pause in speech: Why it matters*. The Speaker Lab. https://thespeakerlab.com/blog/pause-in-speech/

Sprout Social. (n.d.). *Inclusive language guidelines*. Sprout Social Inc. https://seeds.sproutsocial.com/writing/inclusive-language/

Stiegler, M. (2020). *The importance of public speaking for career advancement*. Marjorie Stiegler MD. http://marjoriestieglermd.com/the-importance-of-public-speaking-for-career-advancement/

The Institute of Skills. (n.d.). *The hero's journey in public speaking*. The Institute of Skills. https://theinstituteofskills.com/the-heros-journey-in-public-speaking/#:~:text=In%20the%20context%20of%20public,feels%20familiar%20and%20emotionally%20resonant.

Toastmasters International. (n.d.). *The benefits of Toastmasters membership*. https://www.toastmasters.org/resources/the-benefits-of-toastmasters-membership

Waite, R. (2024). *Public speaking: 7 reasons why leaders must master this skill*. Robin Waite. https://www.robinwaite.com/blog/public-speaking-7-reasons-why-leaders-must-master-this-skill#:~:text=Key%20Takeaways%20on%20Why%20Leaders%20Must%20Master%20Public%20Speaking%26text=Create%20Clarity%20in%20Roles%20and,navigate%20their%20tasks%20with%20purpose.

Women Tech Network. (n.d.). *Sheryl Sandberg - Advocating leadership and inclusion*. Women Tech Network. https://www.womentech.net/how-to/sheryl-sandberg-advocating-leadership-and-inclusion

www.ingramcontent.com/pod-product-compliance
Lightning Source LLC
Chambersburg PA
CBHW071244070526
44583CB00017B/2316